# Homage to

# MARINO MARINI

# HOMAGE TO MARINO MARINI

## Special issue of the XX<sup>e</sup> siècle Review
## Edited by G. di San Lazzaro

**Tributes:**

Marino as a Roman (*Paul Fierens*). Marini and Boccioni (*Eduard Trier*). The Love of Form (*Filippo De Pisis*). First Stay in Switzerland (*Gianfranco Contini*). Space and Form (*Raffaele Carrieri*). A Threatened Civilization (*Lamberto Vitali*). The Themes of Marini (*Enzo Carli*). Making a Portrait (*A. M. Hammacher*). A Plastic Dramatization (*Werner Hofmann*). A Witness of his Time (*Alberto Busignani*). The Élan of the "Warriors" (*Franco Russoli*). The Painter and the Sculptor (*Franco Russoli*). The Contemporary Relevance of Marini (*Umbro Apollonio*). The Lithographs (*Douglas Cooper, Giovanni Carandente*). The Engravings (*Franco Russoli*). The Meaning of an Œuvre (*Carlo Pirovano*).

**An original lithograph by Marino Marini**

*Layout by Christine Gintz*
*Translated by Wade Stevenson*

© by XX<sup>e</sup> siècle, Paris. Printed in Italy by Amilcare Pizzi, Milan. ISBN 8148-0594-9

## TUDOR PUBLISHING COMPANY - NEW YORK

(Photo Marina Marini)

# Prologue to a Premonition

When the ominous wave of Hitlerism was sweeping over Europe, Paul Valéry reminded us that civilizations are mortal. In fact, they are not only mortal, they are also inevitable. What would Europe be today, from what civilization would it descend, if it were not for the battles of Thermopylae, Roman Cannes, or, closer to us, Poitiers? But between one civilization and another there are often long interregnums, so to speak, a sort of spiritual no man's land in which everything seems to plunge into a darkness that can last for centuries before something new is slowly crystallized. The anguish that is expressed in the work of Marino Marini is related, it seems to me, not to the end of the world, but to that of a civilization, to everything bequeathed to us by the past and that we have loved since our childhood, and to the inevitable no man's land that will follow it. A victim of science, of technology, of the class struggle and the police state, our old world is coming apart. It is not just unravelling like a bad piece of fabric but is actually collapsing, coming apart on the inside as much as on the outside.

Marino Marini, in his sculpture as well as in his painting, has never concerned himself with historic events. He never painted Guernica or Massacres in Korea. *He is a man of symbols. Since the beginning of time the horse has been a universal symbol of energy and the vital instinct. Here then is a body of work that has always refrained from finding its inspiration in external events, and yet, by premonitory signs, it still foretold some of the most bitter aspects of contemporary history. It did this in the very course of its development, from the first almost academic marbles to the tragedy inherent in the most recent stones, by way of the glorious series of bronzes and sculpted woods.*

*Marino Marini's work follows a straight, continuous line that is never untrue to itself. Its behavior is similar to that of a plant or of man. In it can be found the smile of adolescence, the blossoming and the beauty of young forms, the drama of middle age, the tragedy of old age. Obviously, what interests us above all is his perfect mastery of technique—of sculpture as well as of painting—, his vigor, his genius. This is to be taken especially in relation to the unconscious or the particular philosophy of the artist.*

*XX$^e$ siècle is honored to have followed the work of Marino Marini since its first issue (1938) and feels obliged to pay him this homage at a time when the official world is beginning to realize the magnitude of his greatness.*

G. DI SAN LAZZARO

I would like to thank Mrs. Marino Marini, Mr. Arturo Bassi, and all those whose efficient collaboration made this book possible.

3

# Homage to Marino Marini

## by Jacques Lassaigne

In Milan's new Museum of Modern Art (Galleria Civica d'Arte Moderna), six rooms are devoted to the work of Marino Marini. This could not be more fitting, as it gives the artist at last the place he deserves at the head of contemporary sculpture. Marini contributed to the homage paid him by making a donation to the museum of an important series of "Portraits" which were exhibited in Milan a few years ago under the title "Personages of the 20th Century."

Although there are good examples of his work in private collections abroad as well as in many major museums (the Tate Gallery, London, the National Gallery, Berlin, the Kunstmuseum, Basel, the Kunsthaus, Zurich, the Museum of Modern Art, New York, and the National Gallery of Canada, Ottawa), the Musée National d'Art Moderne in Paris possesses only a rather mediocre terracotta of 1929 (*Portrait of Gaby*). The Italian museums, with the exception of the Galleria Nazionale d'Arte Moderna in Rome, also appear to ignore him. Apart from the works exhibited at the Palazzo Venezia in Rome in 1966, the most important work of Marini was, until now, the *Large Rider* erected on the Grand Canal in front of the residence that became the Peggy Guggenheim Museum. Marini has simply not had the big international retrospectives that he deserves, and in this sense the presentation on his behalf made by the Museum in Milan is particularly opportune.

As is generally the case with great sculptors, Marino Marini has developed a few essential and familiar themes that in spite of his hard work he has never exhausted. These themes are rather varied and owe nothing to any mode. One of their aspects is the extraordinary series of portraits that the artist made of the men and women who surrounded him, in particular the great painters and sculptors of his generation, whether Italian or foreign (for example, Henry Moore or Germaine Richier) to whom he addresses the same fraternal interrogation. Others are simply collectors, friends or women to whom he was close, as well as anonymous human types whose characters are no less accentuated and whom he places under the general title of *People*.

Like Rodin and Maillol, Marini found in the female body an inexhaustible source of inspiration. Undoubtedly he prefers the rounded fullness of the *Pomonas*, but he also loves the quick, thrusting motion of a dancing figure whose taut, arched forms are projected into space, as his important drawings attest.

On the other side of his creation are the figures that belong to the third series of his work, perhaps the most original, that deals with the theme of the *Warriors*. These are isolated soldiers or riders who, like centaurs, are merged with their horses. They are invariably attached to the ground or form a particular angle with it that corresponds to their internal structure and tension.

In spite of what one might think, these last figures are free of any trace of archaism. Etruscan art comes to mind, which was also so rich in horses and riders, or Donatello. But that is anecdotal. What is important is that Marini's sculpture develops a sort of multiple unity. One thinks of Sluter's *Monks* whose clothes unfold as if they were actual extensions of their bodies.

Clearly Marini nourished his art on many traditions of which his own work is a natural prolongation. But he had no need to reject any of them to affirm his own originality and power. In the same way it is its structure that makes his work monumental, not its real size; some of his smallest works and sketches are gigantesque. Yet at the same time his economy of means preserves him from excess and grandiloquence. In the universe of Marini everything is in its right place. The creature is affirmed by its verticality. Its hooves arched on the ground, the horse is ready to take any leap.

Out of the development of Marini's sculpture there comes a strange wisdom. It has grown and blossomed and acquired a serene confidence in itself. Possibly one day it will fall asleep so that it can be rediscovered by future generations and reveal to them the secret of our best truth.

# Thoughts of Marino Marini on Art and Artists

### The Situation of the Artist and the Quality of the Work

What gives a work of art its modeling and its structure if it is not the release of the vital impulse?

I reacted to Fascism and the imperialist pathos of its artistic directives by identifying my artistic conscience and my private life. In this way I avoided everything that might have been too representational. This is also why I did busts that resemble those anonymous funeral portraits which are free of any trace of historical pathos. Two thousand years have gone by and we are still deeply moved by the human presence that is incarnate in them.

I don't believe there is any need for the artist to worry about more or less ephemeral theories that are constantly changing. If the artist succeeds in creating a work, it is because the alliance of his inspiration and his technical ability necessarily lead to the solution of the problem. Besides, if there is a problem, it is always different. The only thing that matters is the quality of the work.

As for myself, since I am a Mediterranean, I can express myself freely only through the human. But I accept and admire every other form of expression provided it faithfully communicates the message of the artist. A match may be more moving than a Doric column, but it would be ridiculous to concede a priori that a matchbox might constitute a message on the same level of importance as the Parthenon.

I make no distinction between abstract and figurative art, as long as in either case it's truly a question of art.

The existence of a work of art is linked to its participation in both figurative and abstract forms of expression. These two elements come together to create life. Now that's what art is all about!

Perhaps it is the tragic feeling of our time that has caused my work to develop in a tragic way.

Even in states of complete serenity I have always felt that this serenity could not last.

It is strange to think that in the marvelous space God has created, man chooses small paths for himself. After this, all of the humanity around

Female Nude. 1932. India ink drawing. Civica Raccolta Stampe Bertarelli, Milan.

(Photo Herbert List)

I have always felt a need to paint. Besides, I never begin a sculpture without first undertaking pictorial researches in order to feel its vital necessity.

Painting is born like a spontaneous need and thrives on the appetite for color. There is no sculpture if you first don't go through this spiritual state.

Painting, for me, depends on color, which takes me further and further away from real form. The emotion that colors awake in me, that is to say the contrast of one color with another, or their relationship, stimulates my imagination much more than does the materialization of the human figure if I have to rely on pictorial means alone.

## Materials

I have no preference for one "material" over another. In an absolute sense, the material I use really makes no difference. It is the artist who gives each material life. I am completely against the kind of idealist and historicist criticism that insists, for example, that Michelangelo could not possibly have used fragments of Roman marble with double or triple veins instead of a marble that was extra fine and perfect. As if an artist had

The Concept of the Rider. 1955. India ink drawing. Geert van der Veen Coll., Otterlo.

him nourishes him with an infinite number of things.

"Simplifying" does not really lead away from nature but toward it. Nature herself is a great simplifier. The dissolved, destroyed forms, the human figures, the prostrate horses, the debris scattered on the ground, the fragments of flesh, become matter again. What was shapeless is regiven shape. These fallen masses ask to be reestablished; these forms in decay long for revival as solid and whole masses. Reality is form, as the bone-structure holds up the flesh. It thus escapes from chance. Isn't this the path that leads to abstraction?

## Painting and Color

For me, conceiving a form is equivalent to perceiving a color. The vision of color, the ardor of life, the ardor of form, are all related. I have always looked for the starting point of the idea—of any idea capable of becoming a reality—in color. Painting is entering the poetry of action, and action, as it takes place, becomes "true."

to have a preference for a "material." Isn't it the artist who creates the value of the "material" and not the contrary?

I like almost all materials. At bottom, it suffices to understand the material to know how it should be worked. This is true even for plaster, which is only provisory. Even sand.

When I am working with bronze, the more I brutalize it, the more I violate it, the more the mysterious patina emerges. Beautiful and natural.

It is reported that Donatello attacked bronze directly. It is a real joy to work a surface that is so hard and dense, to chisel it, to impart life to a form that is practically dead when it comes out of the casting process.

You realize that there's something that no longer belongs to you. And so you attack your bronze again, you rough it up, you take a hammer and you hit it. And your bronze becomes alive. And the more you hit it, the more it lives.

## Art and History

Since my ancestors were Etruscan, I wanted to free myself of their influence and go further. The elements that have been most stimulating for my work come from Egyptian art.

(*Photo Herbert List*)

Horse and Rider. 1941. India ink drawing. Philadelphia Museum of Art.

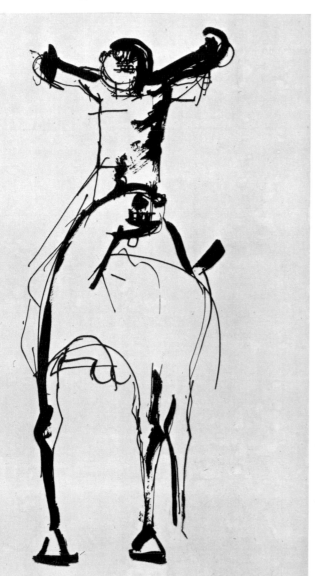

And the Gothic artists? Finally, one always returns to them. We are so attached to that vital center. Gothic art represents an ideal civilization that came to us by way of Byzantium. Donatello finally enters the realm of human reality. As for Giovanni Pisano, he blossoms in it like an aureole around the sun. His work is marked by both precision and imprecision. In art, a great imprecision is sometimes more important than a precision that is too precise.

A new civilization is one that bears enough warmth within itself to live and survive for centuries. It is precisely because he always set out from the roots that Donatello has always interested me, not, of course, for the principle but for his accomplishments. Nonetheless, I wanted to discover the process of his development. Donatello "saw" the Romans. The visible proof of this is the proportions of his heads, the movement of his hands. Through the intermediary of the Romans, he succeeded in creating a distinctive physiognomy. As for myself, I went back to the world of the Etruscans in order to find my own.

If we admire ancient art, it is because of its

Miracle. 1969. Pen-and-ink drawing.

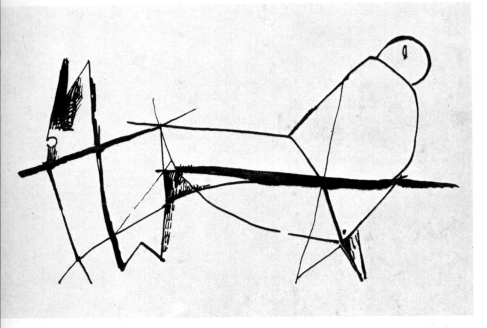

Warrior. 1969. Pen-and-ink drawing.

The Cry. 1969. Pen-and-ink drawing.

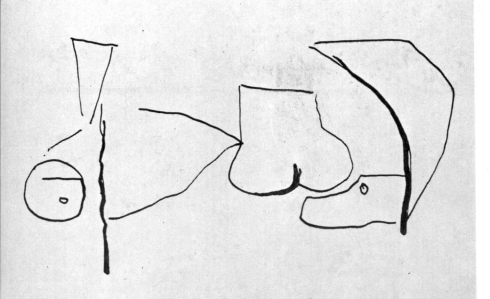

virility, not its sense of composition. The almost cylindrical form is like the sun on the earth, isn't it? This is what interested me the most, thanks to which I'm fully involved in the problem.

### The Bamberg Rider

I have always been attracted by the North. The North, for me, represents something very positive. Since I come from the South and am so aware of Italian values, I feel the need for a contrast.

During the course of my travels in Italy, whether to Rome, Venice or Padua, I never was moved by equestrian monuments. But Bamberg, in Germany, made a deep impression on me. Probably because it is the fruit of a fabulous, remote world, in a lost country.

### The Portraits

The first thing I see is a form, a profile. It's round or it's elongated. These are the essential data it's necessary to become aware of. Next I try to enter into the spirit of the person I'm portraying. That's the difficult part: imagining this face in a human context, that is, in keeping with a criterion common to other men. This done, that's all there is to it. This truth must continue to live in me in such a way that the work I do is fully a portrait. I am only satisfied with the result if it expresses both the singularity and the "archetype" of the person. Once this task has been accomplished the subject then assumes his place in the world of the dead who have come to life again, and at last I hand my work over.

A certain length of time may elapse between the moment when I begin a portrait and the moment when I take it up again to complete it. I am not a methodical or "predetermined" kind of artist, although nothing is left to chance.

Some people are certainly more interesting and alive than others. For example: Stravinsky, Chagall, Germaine Richier. Each of them interested me for their own personal, well-defined characteristics. Stravinsky, for example, was a lively, nervous, apprehensive kind of character, and what interested me precisely was the vital force that emanated from him, a force that was wholly made up of sensitivity and that gave me great difficulties but also great joy. Then there was Chagall, a kind of crazy lover, in love with color; the vivacity of his artistic expression was reflected in his physical structure; it was something that was not easy to render: it was another very interesting field for the imagination to explore. Miller is a person who, when I tried to seize him, flowed away in every direction; he couldn't be captured. I had to imagine him, to corner him, to shut him up in a way; I was given ten minutes to "realize" him, so to speak, and I still don't know how I did it.

Every woman presents herself to the artist in a certain way. Through his study of her the artist

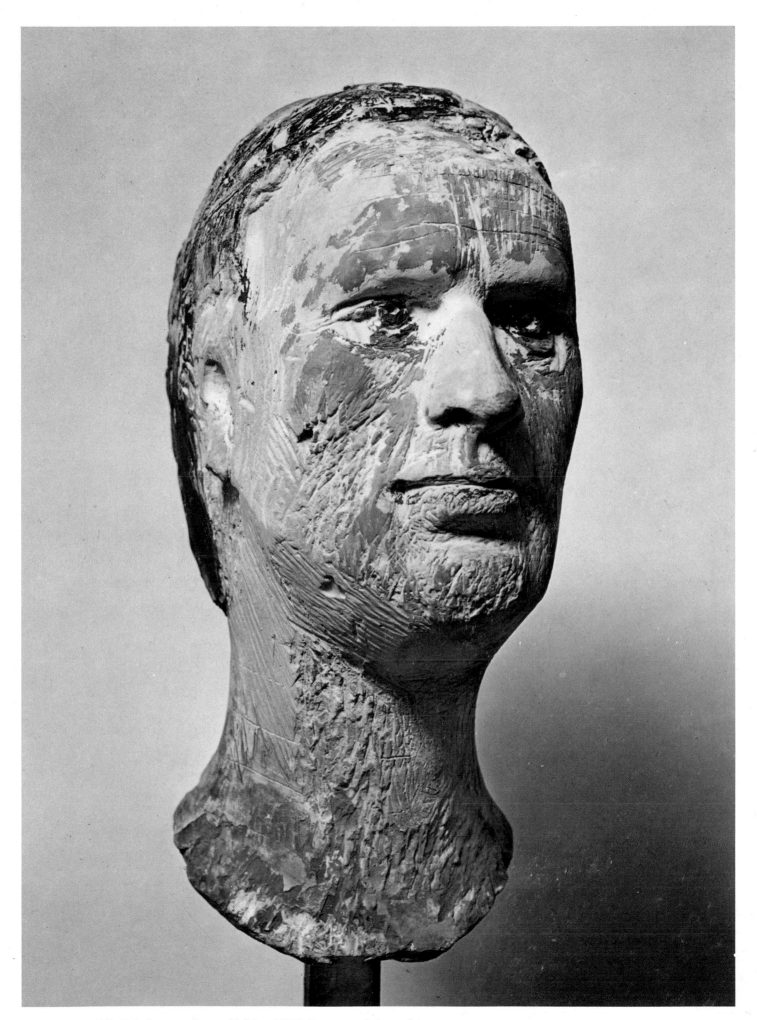

Self-Portrait. 1942. Polychrome plaster. Height: 16 1/8". Property of the artist.

succeeds in defining and creating a reality that the woman herself does not imagine, or that she is aware of but seeks to hide. Man is more natural and shows himself as he is; woman reveals herself less.

### The Pomonas

In all these images (the *Pomonas*), femininity is enriched with the most ancient, immanent and mysterious values. They embody a sort of ineluctable necessity, of motionless fixity, of primitive and unconscious fecundity.

### Horses and Riders

If you look at my equestrian statues of the last twelve years one after the other, you can see that each time the rider is less capable of mastering his mount and that the horse, in its anguish, becomes even more savage and intractable instead of yielding. I seriously believe that we are approaching the end of a world.

When I say this, my state of mind is close to that of the Romans who, at the end of the Empire, watched a century-old order collapse under the impact of the barbarian invasions. My equestrian statues express the torment caused by the events of this century. The uneasiness expressed by my horses increases with each new version; as for the rider, he is always more tired. He has lost his authority over his mount, and the disasters to which he succumbs resemble those that destroyed Sodom and Pompeii. What I want to do is to portray the last stage in the dissolution of a myth, of the myth of the heroic and victorious individual, of the "uomo di virtù" of the humanists. My works of these past fifteen years have not wanted to be heroic, but tragic.

### The Miracles

The fallen riders become the *Miracles*. They destroyed themselves. They became ashes. Ashes that nonetheless have a structure.

I am attracted by the sky. I no longer feel well on the earth. I would like to enter the cosmos or make a hole in the earth's crust. I'm no longer able to feel peaceful among men, who, besides, are not very peaceful themselves. The horse falls down and the rider is thrown, as in the *Miracles*.

### The Warriors

The *Warriors* exist only in one reality. A single vision, tragic and passionate, without any possibility of joy, encompasses them.

*These "Thoughts" have been taken from interviews and especially from the one that served as the introduction to the catalogue of the exhibition "Personaggi del XX secolo" at the Centro Studi Piero della Francesca in Milan, 1972.*

Three Female Nudes. 1950. Pen-and-ink drawing. 13″ × 9 ¹/₂″. Riccardo Jucker Coll., Milan.

Jean Arp. 1963. Crayon and watercolor.
12 ¹/₂″ × 9 ³/₈″. Galleria Civica d'Arte Moderna, Milan.

# In Milan, about 1930

## by André Pieyre de Mandiargues

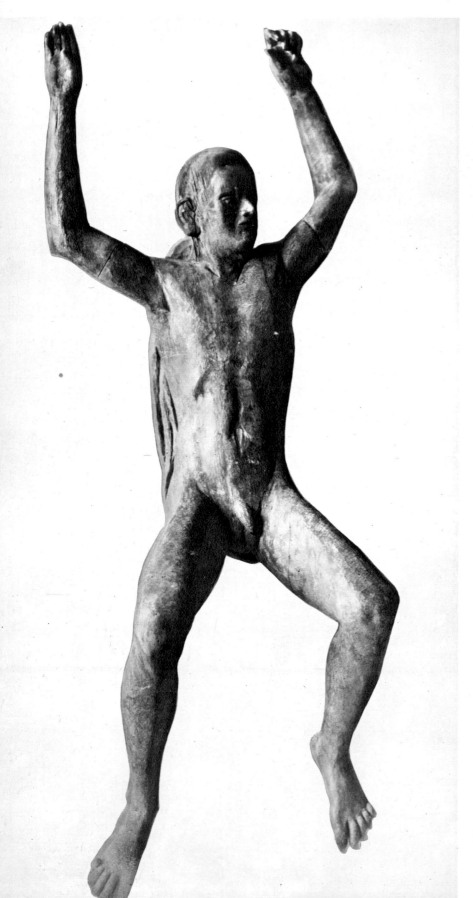

It was in the spring of 1932, ten days before Easter, to be precise. I remember having loaded my car under a dark sky at Brigue to go through the Simplon tunnel, and then, on the sunny quay of the train station at Domodossola, unloading it and taking the top down at once. Then I took the road that runs in front of the shabby inn where Musset lived and drove toward Lake Maggiore and a Milan which at that time was neoclassical and impregnated with romanticism. There were not many cars in the streets, and above the noise of their motors the music of hand organs could be heard and violets were on sale just about everywhere. Thus the pleasures of hearing were merged with those of smell, and there was the promise of good food in cool restaurants. Soon I had met many of the artists who belonged to the *Novecento* group and who were responsible for most of what was important in Italian painting and sculpture at that time. Although the word "discovery" is a little embarrassing, I use it without hesitation to describe my meeting with Marino Marini and my visit to his studio.

I knew many painters from the period in question, but no sculptors. At that point in my life I was lazily studying archaeology and had Etruscan art on my mind, and sculpture was something that seemed to belong in museums. But suddenly those Etruscans from the past came to life and vividly erupted in my mind, and this was due to my visit to the studio of the young Tuscan sculptor. His face had a fine arched smile that is still his natural expression and that would be as naturally in place on the statue of a god two thousand years old. Should I add that the Etruscan smile, like that of the Pre-Columbian heads from the region of Vera-Cruz, is not necessarily a sign of gaiety, but rather represents a kind of superior serenity before the problems of life, death, pleasure, suffering and art which is a trifle Nietzschean and is perhaps not devoid of some incisive cruelty? Yes... And doesn't this incisive cruelty fit in exactly with Weininger's idea of the sculptor? Yes again... And here I must add that at the time I had just finished reading Weininger in the Italian translation that exerted such an influence on the artists of the *Novecento*; I still wonder, by the way, when it will be possible to read *Sex and Character* in French. But let us return to Marino.

Icarus. 1933. Wood. Height: 70 7/8".
Battiato Coll., Milan.

Marino Marini ... Has anyone noticed how this name, which in keeping with an old and charming Italian usage (for example, Castruccio Castracana) has a kind of double-barrelled impact as if to better shoot down, like a pheasant, the art critic or the simple art lover—has anyone ever noticed how it quickly folds up into the first name? The day when, in the company of friends who introduced me, I entered Marino Marini's studio for the first time, I already spoke of him as Marino. And Marino, when he showed us his works with measured gestures whose gentleness did not exclude a certain hardness that is as Tuscan as the Etruscan smile, made me understand the substance of his art and the kind of artist that he was as easily as this was shown to me fifteen years later by the great Germaine Richier. Richier admired Marino very much. It seemed to me that she was happy to learn that I admired him too and that I owed him my initiation into the world of their work: the most intimidating, if not the most difficult, of all the arts, and perhaps the most private (the least accessible) as well, sculpture.

Sometimes I wonder whether, among all the activities of man, there are any that prostitute themselves less than sculpture? Almost none.

I still have not forgotten the works that Marino showed us that day. I remember a few heads, mostly portraits, that impressed me at first glance by the just simplicity with which they set the face of man in space and defined the space around it. They were heads, not busts, although there probably was some chest and a more or less ravaged spine below. The *busto*, in Italian, is also a corsage and a corset, and Marino is well aware of this. His lesson is that sculpture has no relationship with passementerie and that it is, on the contrary, a stripping bare, a casting off with a view to rigorous inspection and description in the three dimensions that are its essence. In this respect Marino readily considers himself to be the exact opposite of an Italian sculptor whom I admire unreservedly, Bernini. Bernini's busts are busts in the worst sense of the word, which does not keep them from being extraordinary because of the secret of the artist. His secret consists in condemning his model to death by dressing it in ribbons and lace carved in the whitest Carrara marble. Marini's secret is the contrary of the baroque master's. So much the better for both, and their ability to raise contrary signs to a degree of absolute intensity. What is positive is like what is negative, it is only a question of terminology. When we judge the tension that dwells in a work, as if we actually touched it, it is the violence of the felt shock that is our means of measurement.

Even more than the heads in bronze, clay or plaster, however, I remember a large unfinished wooden statue that still fills me with a sense of wonder. An *Icarus*, sufficiently detached from mythological figuration so as only to represent nudity and an idea of falling in the eyes of an uninformed observer. Among modern sculptors,

Swimmer. 1932. Wood. 45 ¾" × 19 ¾".
Emilio Jesi Coll., Milan.

1  Ersilia. 1931. Polychrome wood. 57 7/8″ × 17 3/8″ × 26 3/4″.
Kunsthaus, Zurich. (Reworked in 1949).

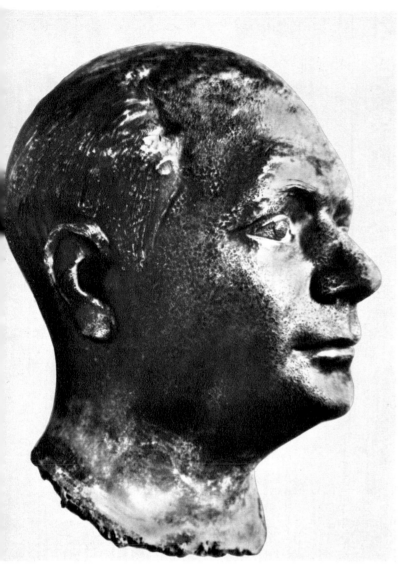

Portrait of Alberto Magnelli. 1929. Bronze. Height: about
12 5/8″. Property of the artist.

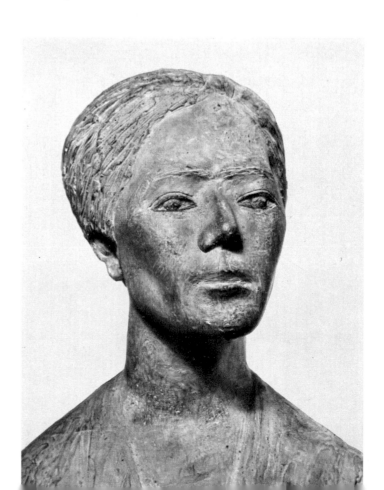

The Bourgeoise. Polychrome terracotta. Height: 14 5/8″. Galleria
Civica d'Arte Moderna, Milan.

Portrait of Gaby. 1932. Terracotta.
Height: 19 3/4″. Musée
National d'Art Moderne, Paris.

Marino is one of the first to have understood
everything that wooden sculpture was capable of
and to have restored to this art or to this material
the dignity that the primitives alone bestowed on
it. Because wood is the most living of the materials a sculptor uses, a long struggle takes place
between the creator and the intractable creature
(or creation) that must, so to speak, be slowly
tortured to death before the work can be completed; finally, it is considered only as a means
relative to the stable ideal in which the sculptor
wishes to fix it. *Icarus* still seemed to be alive
while in front of us Marino hollowed, carved,

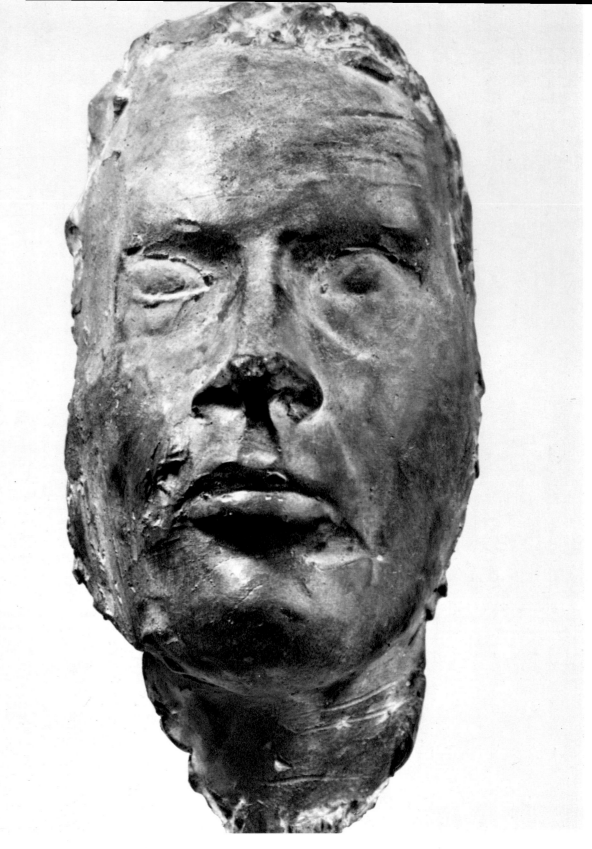

Self-Portrait. 1935. Bronze. Height: 10 ¼". Emilio Jesi Coll., Milan.

shaved and polished its body in a masterly fashion. I have no need to say more as the sense in which I speak here of the master is self-explanatory.

But the most surprising thing, perhaps, still remains to be said. For today it seems to me that in playing with murder or in caressing death, as I have tried to describe, Marino on that April morning in Lombardy gave me the most beautiful lesson of love and even, quite simply, of life that I have ever received.

16

# In the Serene Shadow

## by Egle Marini

Marino was born as a Mediterranean in the Tyrrhenian basin, an ancient land where, among the shadows of those who lovingly cultivated it, the serene presence of Giotto, the emaciated humanity of Masaccio, the uneasiness of Pisano, can still be felt. He was born, to be precise, in the peaceful early part of this century at Pistoia, a stony medieval city built on the rocks very close to the Apennines. Black and white marble structures surmounted by the grin of gargoyles are embedded in its architecture. A plain and a hill surround it; in the distance lies Florence; above is the great parabola of the sun and the absolute presence of the night, so quiet one can hear a dormouse breathing in the shadows of the buildings. But above all there is the sensation of time, the slowness of time.

Fragments of images from childhood have remained printed on the retina, each with their own color, their particular chiaroscuro:

"The walls of the house around us like arms. The red stove, a pair of small chairs, four hands in the warmth of a lap: a feeling of something very strong, like a shelter, a grotto. The smell of an oil lamp, the blue flame sticking out a little stammering tongue into the glass tube. Both of us huddling in the chair, my brother's smock that smells of school. The flat candlestick that moves through the shadow-filled rooms; sleeping with your fists closed. Frosty mornings that fall down brutally on closed eyelids, the cold shower on your back like the blow of a whip, and then school and time slowly ticking away like a pendulum. How sad the desks look and how gray the windows! Duties. Sundays and their ritual processions. The long prayers in the evening for the Dead ... The bright toys. The red medication. The red wheel of the car."

Like a fruit swelling under the thrust of sap, Marino grew up in this orderly universe: a slow, rich growth, interrupted by ardent explosions. Marino was a taciturn child, quick to laugh; he was as indifferent to reprimands as he was depressed by school books; he hardly applied himself and mechanically absorbed fragments of Roman history or of a poem whose words stuck in his ear, only in his ear.

His childhood was surrounded by a family solicitude, and since what was allowed and what was forbidden was based on pure feeling alone, it could seem gratuitous. But Marino was a very independent child and he more or less did as he pleased. He rebelled against any systematic approach to learning and instinctively was drawn toward images.

At the age of twelve or fourteen he grew fond of drawing. His geography notebook was filled with clear, well-defined colors and a thin, concise handwriting. He was really most happy when drawing, and his natural physical indocility disappeared when he traced the shape of a continent. Then a certain behavior manifested itself that divided the child: carefully, jealously, he began to store something away in a secret hiding place inside himself.

It was 1914, 1915: the First World War had just

Judith. 1945. Bronze. 53 $\frac{1}{8}$" × 20 $\frac{1}{8}$" × 25 $\frac{5}{8}$". Middelheim Park Museum, Antwerp.

broken out. A climate of rigor and restriction against a gray-green background.

During that period there was also a brief meeting with Rodin. Marino listened to him and the impression was lasting.

In 1917 Marino entered the Academy of Fine Arts in Florence. He had lost nothing of his natural serenity; less silent, even more absorbed, he spent his time drawing, which he loved. And always there were his sudden outbursts of laughter whose trace seemed to remain on his face. Born out of an intimate contact with his native ground, the first notes of color, clear as crystal, sharp as the first sounds in the morning, began to spring up. They had the rhythm of the slow flow of sap that simply and mysteriously was working within him.

There always will be an unconscious reserve in Marino, an instinctive rejection of contact, a repugnance to translate into words the current that runs through him and that escapes, ardent, uneasy, impetuous, only through narrow openings.

In those first works inspired by nature, Marino played with color as with a mosaic: the juxtaposed yellows of a bird's head, the purple and golden meanderings of a corolla, the emerald and jade nuances of insects examined as if they were jewels. The whole was infused with a spirit of transparency and lightness and was, in fact, the transcription of an inner myth.

War was still present. In the gambling rooms, behind sombre colonnades, were piled up the vestiges of a crepuscular Ottocento, cold plaster-works and their drapery, a live, standing model holding a stick as if it were a halberd, and the phantoms of irrevocably dead masters. Between Pistoia and Florence stretched the plain rich with its living gifts, dominated by the imposing mass of the Apennines. There was talk about "Cubism" and "Futurism" in the midst of the continuing war. Old people and adolescents wandered around in a general state of wretchedness, brought together by the vacuum caused by the dead and those who had been mobilized.

In 1918 Marino was, in his own words, a "closed pebble"; would he be mobilized? He tried out his working tools, pursued his individual quest of images outside of the beaten paths that are soon forgotten. Ignoring the technical difficulties, he set out, alert, serene, free, a stranger to slogans, into the truth that was his own. As he progressed his experience grew richer, although the means that he had at his disposal were hardly sufficient to deal with the dynamic force that was inside him. He made use of everything and of nothing. His attentive ears picked up the echoes of ancient civilizations even before he knew of their existence.

There were undoubtedly many deep Mediterranean currents moving within him, the shadows of bare feet, the memories of ancestors whose life still beats in their tombs, the symphony of the rivers and forests gradually cut down by time, the rhythm of oxen moving under the vast tranquil

Venus. 1945. Terracotta. Height: 43 ¼".
Gianni Mattioli Coll., Milan.

The People. 1929. Terracotta. 26″ × 42 $^{15}/_{16}$″ × 18 $^1/_2$″. Galleria Civica d'Arte Moderna, Milan.

Archangel. 1943. Polychrome plaster. Height: 51 ³/₄″. Christoph Bernouilli Coll., Basel.

Juggler. 1944. Polychrome bronze. ▷
Height: 36 ¹/₄″. Property of the artist.

Rider. 1949/51. Polychrome wood. 43 ¹/₄" × 70 ⁷/₈". Kunstverein, Düsseldorf.

Rider. 1947. Bronze. Height: 63 ¾". Boymans van Beuningen Museum, Rotterdam.

skies along the Apennines, the steps of shepherds, the cries of wolves—in short, the whole weight of history. Filtered through architectural structures similar to jewels placed on velvet or set in stone, voices swell up out of a far-reaching expanse of beauty whose modulations are perceptible to a sensitive ear.

1919. The doors of the postwar classrooms swung open again and let the light in. Marino executed his first large canvases. He attended classes where he studied the nude and the techniques of engraving. His drawings demonstrated his intellectual agility and creative dynamism and transcribed the emotion corresponding to each part of their wide-ranging structure.

Florence was now the object of Marino's attention. Having grown up in such a harmonious atmosphere, he unconsciously felt very privileged. Then came the day when, stimulated by the Etruscans, he looked at himself in the mirror.

In 1922, to everyone's general surprise, he enrolled in a sculpture class. This may be seen as the conclusion of a natural development related to some distant warning or as the result of an immediate instinct. The drawings that he piled up, with all their arabesques, resembled the transcription of an inner dream. He found his motif, which seemed to emerge from a remote past, in concise hieroglyphs. Marino flung signs on paper as one scatters seeds, and these signs immediately blossomed in his hand. He would abandon a work, take it up again, put it further away, bring it closer, erase it, scratch it, rethink it and give it life; yet each detail had the freshness associated with birth.

His first period can be compared to the arrival of light on a smooth and happy earth. Later, a sense of man's anguish dug a shadow in it and a different, shaken world came forth that Marino at once wanted to explore: the world of men, that world that Marino needs to touch because he is in

23

Horse. 1947. Bronze. Height: about 39 ³/₈″. Mr. and Mrs. Ralph F. Colin Coll., New York.

love, because it makes him curious, because it both hurts and helps him. He sculpted it in the image of his own needs.

Marino also visited Paris several times during that epoch and it was when he returned from one of those trips, in 1929, that his Florentine period came to an end.

This was because Marino accepted the invitation Martini sent him from Milan to come and teach sculpture at the Villa Reale Art School in Monza. At first, he was not too happy about leaving Florence, but Milan was a dynamic center of activity, and the dreamy plain around it and its tender faded sky also had a particular charm for him. In Milan he felt that he was really in Europe, and from there it was easy to travel to the Northern countries which fascinated him. These voyages did indeed fill him with joy.

"I made this transition smoothly... I absorbed it slowly. The cities in central and southern Italy are magnificent, but they are isolated and the values that they live on belong to the past." Or else: "Each artist has his own intuitions, his own

hypersensitivity. I always felt that I had to go to the North, which for me is the positive pole. Saturated with the South and our own Italian values, I felt the need for a contrast, and this contrast, for me, is the North. It's the North that gives you your value, your color. Then there is a genuine nordic experience that makes one aware that an artist has begun to live in the North and to taste its climate. For example, the desolate face of the *Miracle* in Basel came out of my impression of a country whose mountains resemble organ pipes: their music is very different from what I could hear in Italy."

Marino's work, and undoubtedly Marino himself, might be defined as a vibration of silence, a movement in the midst of stasis, a warmth like a burning human breath. Marino's own inner ferments are hidden beneath an open nature. His character might be compared to a smooth and silent river whose sudden eddies reveal a secret and profound strength that is steadily growing in force.

In wood, in stone, in the dry friability of plaster,

his chisel digs, leaves its imprint, imparts life. Behind there is Marino, sober, dynamic, ardent. His face expresses the same hard tension that is embodied in his horses.

The Florentine period was marked by concentration and research, and Marino has not forgotten the confused mixture of impulses and doubts that characterized it. "It was a period that was a little dark, vague, that corresponded to the complexity of a phase of fermentation filled with many questions that were not clearly defined ... Many things were in the process of happening but they could not, perhaps, be all assimilated at once. There was a multitude of ideas jostling among each other, of feelings, of limitations; there were things that were real, things that were thought, things that were imagined, and they were all mixed up in a very imprecise way. They cleared up when I got to Milan which is, even today, the only Italian city that is a part of Europe. The climate there is a European one, and one feels the same things that one would in England, France or Germany. People live in a modern way, everyone is responsible for his work ... It's a true world, based on reality, the only one that's worth anything."

The works that date from the first ten years in Milan are broadly conceived from a formal point of view and represent a progressive human deepening that is full of a controlled, measured vitality. Occasionally a brusque stop, a kind of trembling, betrays the richness of the underlying contents, in the manner of a door that, prudently opened a crack, reveals unsuspected riches.

The drawings announce the acrobats, the horses and riders, the dancers and jugglers; their contours are traced by an intense, fluid line that every now and then is interrupted by an intimately perceived sensation.

After the splendor of the young *Venuses* who resemble bright columns from some Doric temple, and the silent resonances of the *Pomonas*, Marino's work developed in an essentially tragic way. However, this did not happen in an immediate or overt manner. In approaching its goal, which gradually drew nearer, the artist's sensibility followed a rectilinear path. Suddenly, like a handful of scattered seed, a dry, brutal gesture appeared in the vast rhythm, in the wavy amplitude of the forms. Like a burn, it may be thought of as a brief allusion to the rich but reticent world of the artist's inner development. It seems to alight on the ecstatic gracefulness of *Gentleman on a Horse* (1937) and to underline its fragility, its wavering instability and seraphic unconsciousness.

This fissure, this tear, grew constantly larger and soon had spread out to the dancers, jugglers and riders; it even attacked the nucleus, nourished with Etruscan sap, of the successive representations of the female figure.

In 1940, just as World War II was declared, Marino was appointed to a professorship in sculpture at the Brera Academy. Marino felt the shock and withdrew silently into himself. It was as if

Pomona. 1949. Bronze. Height: 66 ⅛".
Statens Museum for Kunst, Copenhagen.

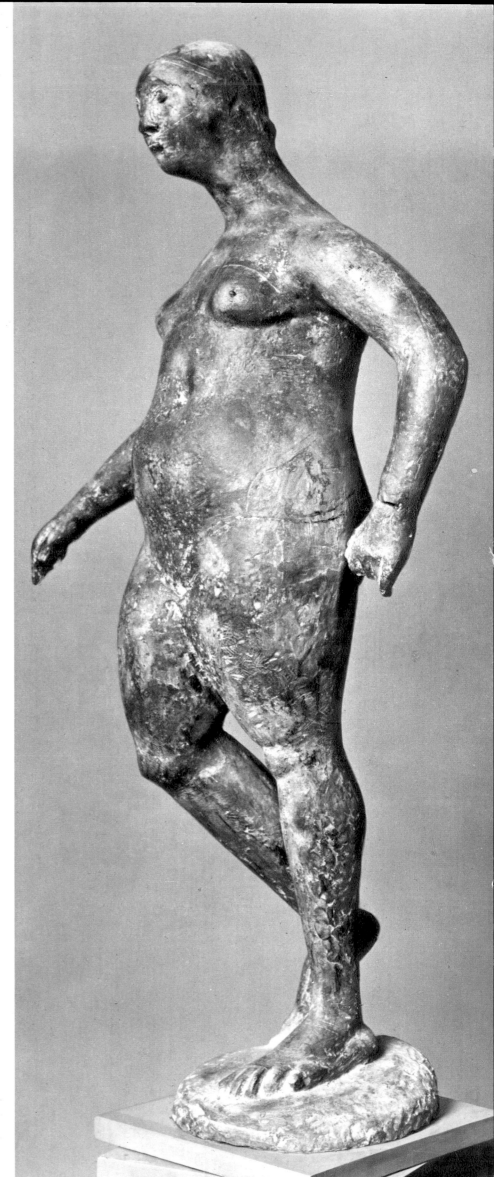

Juggler. 1940. Bronze. Height: 26 ³/₈″ × 16 ¹/₈″ × 31 ¹/₂″. Property of the artist.

the muffled noises of the departing troops had veiled with their shadow the clear light of his new world.

His anguish was soon given expression in his horses, and the look of the rider gave a rhythm to the illusion of a willed dream that derived its power from reality. Simultaneously, however, the theme of the woman continued to affirm itself, expressing contrary values or a necessary questioning, or simply the need Marino felt to open a wide parenthesis. And yet an ambiguous resonance began to emerge in the dancers around 1949—I am thinking of the one whose ardent expressiveness cannot keep one from forgetting the curve of her haunches, or the one whose excessively rich vibrations cannot be bent to the rhythm of the dance. These women are more than just light: they advance, virile, modelled by the shadow, born perhaps from the painful wounds inscribed on the 1943 works (*Miracle, Archangel, Arcangela*); the same holds true for the wandering riders who advance in the wind and rain, stupefied, blinded by their huge shadow, like heroes deprived of reason, heroes of no one; or the riders whose limbs have been lopped off and who, savagely defying emptiness, sit on horses whose necks are flattened out in fear and whose straining nostrils seem to exhale ashes.

Marino did many frenzied variations on this theme, now insisting on the dazed condition of a being condemned to struggle unremittingly, now on the vengeful awakening, the leap forward; in both cases, the emotional charge manages to absorb itself in the internal structure of the work without breaking the line. True, on the large planes of the horse-rider couple Marino sometimes indicates a contrary action, a trembling. The bruise is inscribed in the center of a calm certainty and has been carefully thought out and restrained by the reserve and measure of the artist whose emotivity carries on a dialogue with itself and constitutes, so to speak, its own refuge.

But the emotive charge does find a release in the vertical riders and in the *Miracles* in which a desperate quest for an outlet can be seen—as if it were ready to leap over the world as in dreams—and it explodes in the unseated and derisory *Warriors* who are crushed and buried beneath their own mass, and in the ravaged *Cry* in which the rider is crumpled under the impact of destruction. The interrogation here is so anguished that it leads to the question: is a reconstruction possible?

Henceforward, form, considered as light, is not victorious over the shadow or the wound; rather, the wound has taken on form and in fact has become form.

Marino, his character excepted, is still turned inward on himself, just as he was in his childhood when, preferring images to words, he ripened in himself and out of his own personality.

Sometimes a tremor in his look spreads to his face whose sensitive expression it accentuates before losing itself, imperceptibly, at his fingertips. The concept of the work stays intact inside him where it develops in subterranean, unfathomable ways. "You must not describe a project; if you do, you lose it."

The restrained emotion visible in the *Pomonas* burst out in full force when Marino's works were brought together at the Palazzo Venezia in Rome. Immense and surprising, these powerful creatures assert themselves by a mute vibration. Next to each other, facing each other, their warm breaths are mixed together in a dialogue full of élans and reticences. If in the past, during the serene period, they were marked already by the sign of shadow, they now appear like a smile in the heart of the shadow that has invaded the entire work.

Bare and tragic, the form is split in the prostrated riders and horses of the *Miracles*, angels petrified by terror, fixed in their trembling, and as if still struck by lightning, which tattoes them with its cinders and fire.

The role once played by the *Venuses* and the earthly *Pomonas* was taken over as of 1950 by the nervous, vibrant dancers as well as by the acrobats that succeeded the *Seated Juggler* (1944) whose shivering and uneasy ambiguity raises it to a pitch of the highest tension. They also show us the bright side of Marino's work at the very moment

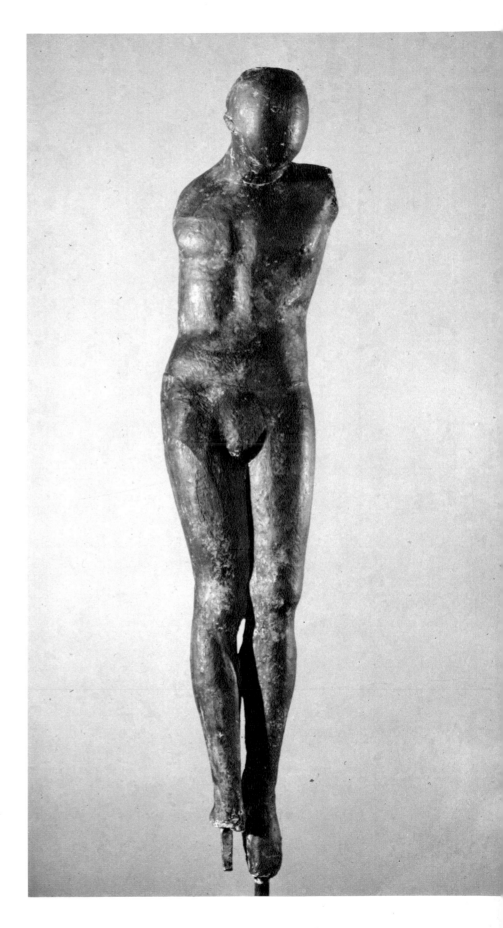

Juggler. 1946. Bronze. Height: 72 $^1/_{16}$". Kunsthaus, Zurich. (Gift of W. and N. Bär).

Rider. 1951. Bronze. Height: about 45 ¼". Union of Industrial Workers, Stockholm. (*Photo Bo Boustedt*).

when, in the other sculptures, the architecture was collapsing and the material disintegrating.

Would the work succeed in being reborn out of its ashes?

During the long march toward a constructive harmony, emotion made grief reappear.

On what was a final convulsion, love can impose anachronistic signs.

The peace and even the linearity that arise out of the remains of an absolute destruction can culminate in an intact, saved essence that has an original purity. Now it is up to color to show us, on the theme of a painted theater, the clear face of his work by means of the magic of hues and the vibration of its contents. Today, for Marino, the new reality is the shadow that was narrowly enclosed in the disturbing clairvoyance of the female representation of 1972. A reality nourished on a supreme experience, which is birth and acceptance of an *afterwards*, a representation that resembles time and yet is intemporal ... charged with the light that was accumulated with such difficulty in the shadow and which it is now ready to pour out freely.

A reality, finally, that is impermeable to the external reality that surrounds it, a reality that no fire can attack and that nothing can tear away from truth and silence.

# The Attraction of the North

## by J. P. Hodin

### Marini and the Etruscans

There is something quite unique about Marino Marini's personality. If one watches him at work or in a moment of leisure, walking along with friends and discussing some problem of life or art or sitting in the company of women what strikes me as a constant picture is his positiveness. He is supple like an acrobat, his mind reacts to every challenge with an assurance of inner strength and conviction which comes from the heart and the elemental goodness of his complex nature. The features are open, full lips, a wide look from his eyes which, however, can narrow to peppercorn size when sarcasm has to meet an improper intrusion into values which are untouchable for him. Curly rebellious hair crowns his head and there is warmth in his handshake and in his smile. He is as straightforward a man as he is an artist and that is also why it was given to him to find a symbol for man's condition, a symbol as contemporary as it is timeless. Man in his fear, man in his joy, in his aspirations and failures, in his rise, decline and death.

Marini likes to visualize himself as a descendant of the Etruscans and he certainly feels an inner affinity, the invisible pulls at the roots of his being. Born in Pistoia, in the area which was originally Etruscan, this might be true in a purely physical sense as it certainly is in the spiritual sense. "I am Etruscan," he said enthusiastically to me. "The Etruscans were a people stronger than the Greeks, very intelligent. They did not yield to anybody and did not care a rap for anything. They had a spirit, an irony, a vitality which is Northern but Oriental. They were Semitic, they came from the South, the countries of the Jews and the Arabs. Notice their faces. You find types here with small eyes, a sense of the irony of things, careless in their looks, their hair curly."

There was something which one day made me listen and suddenly realize that what once was the fate of a whole race which flourished before the Romans and their civilization, to be finally absorbed by them and which creatively used the impulses from the Greeks both in art and religion, was repeated here in an individual fate again and again, maybe in short periods only but as a certainty anchored in the old experience of the blood. We can find Marini at the height of his humour—

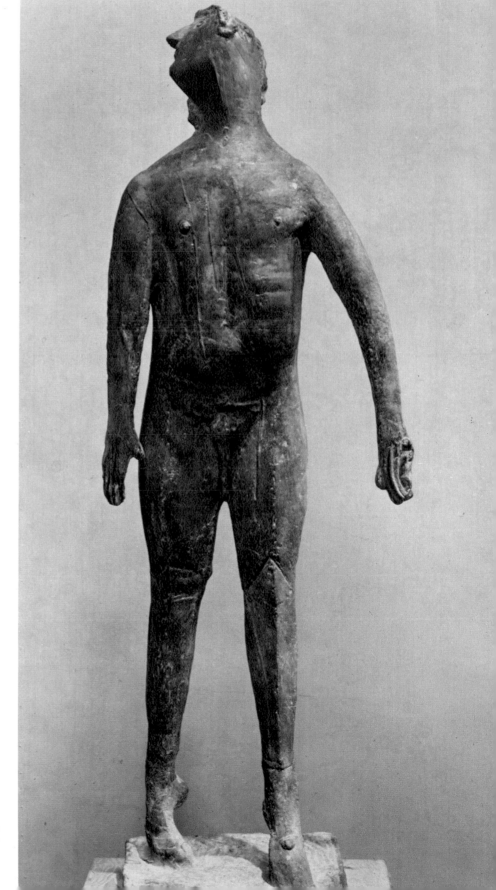

Juggler. 1946. Bronze. Height: 66 ⅛".
Pierre Matisse Gallery, New York.

and there is humour in his mental make-up and a lighthearted acceptance of life as an irreplaceable precious gift full of divine surprises and promises, a grazing ground for his insatiable sensuality, to be enjoyed and treasured—and we can find him melancholy and depressed by man's insufferable bestiality and the pitfalls of his calculating spirit. The sudden realization of the satanic dangers inherent in man's ability to split the atom and to use it for destructive purposes in conjunction with the problem and mentality of our ant-heap over-population can incapacitate him for weeks in the pursuit of—what is his only satisfaction in life— the enrichment of existence by beautiful and meaningful objects which have the power to deepen our love, our sense of the miraculous and our appreciation of existence.

At one time in the history of the Etruscans, the people with the disarming smile and the shrewd eyes of an observant and curious race, as they appear in their sculptures and sepulchral paintings, a people of vigour and serenity, music-lovers and devotees of the dance, imbued with a religiousness which made everyday life appear holy to them for the godhead had penetrated reality and made it divine, both being one and undivisible—suddenly there occurred what so appropriately was called, though in another context, a "Failure of Nerve".[1] From now on everything everywhere stood in the sign of death, the fear and the negation of life and all crafts and skills from now on served its purpose: music, the arts, the code of life, the "discipline" which regulated the relations between men and gods, making man into a mere servant and interpreter of the gods whose powers crushed him. There is an instinctive animal-like quality in Marini, with its rhythm of laziness and tenseness, its uninhibited directness, the joy of life, the alertness of receiving coded messages from it and of reacting in a subtle, often refined, sometimes tragic but always vital and sound manner.

## Modernity and Tradition

Again and again Marini regains his power of balance, a virtue in which he believes, and although the times produce sign after sign which forebode evil he does not fall into the trap of the Existentialist Nihilists like other younger artists by giving way to despair or to the sole acceptance of brutality, violence and fear; he seizes rather upon the wholeness of man's nature and remains a humanist. Therein he is a son of the Mediterranean tradition which created Europe and without which it would lose its soul. This is true of his art as well as of his thought and feeling, the one being the realization of the other.

Being a humanist and not a mere illustrator of abstract scientific notions he never can refrain from the human shape. As man's soul is a whole in all its diversity so is his image. In his depiction of man's spiritual attitudes and emotions Marini

can be called an Expressionist. He once said to me: "Expressionism is a certain moment and a desire for a more accurate conquest particularly in the expression of things, the reassurance of various emotions and of the unity of form and colour." As an Expressionist, Marini avoided the main pitfall of this trend, i.e., of distorting the Realistic form as the only and appropriate means of depicting states of mind. On the contrary, as an executor of tradition and believing necessarily, as a Latin, in order and discipline he introduced on a Cubist basis a constructive element into his art, to force emotion into form. "I regard sculpture as being constructive," he wrote, "and by constructiveness I mean a direction toward the architectural, and the unfolding of an idea which is somewhat remote from the human form and nearer to a constructive and static line." Having started as a draughtsman and painter, Marini the sculptor often returns to this medium, which is organically linked with his artistic vision. "There is a part in me very alive to the graphic expression; the observation is exact in line, the taste for drawing being somehow Nordic. I started to draw very early and my graphic work continues steadily. Painting is born in me as a spontaneous and vivid need in the search for colour. There is no sculptural result if it does not pass through this state of mind. The pictorial objects represented are very often the beginning of a proceeding into sculpture."

Marini's stylistic roots—"I admire all the painting and sculpture of the Primitivists"[2] and his contemporaneity—"For the modern I need time to reflect"—have produced an artist of supreme integrity in whose work one can feel the heartbeat of a human being and genuine empathy. Only in men like Marini can the world reflect itself in all its splendour. He creates the world in which he can live. That is the secret of his personality. "Personality," he says, "is acquired unconsciously in the continuity of poetical experiences reflected in our self."

## Man and Horse

The monument of Marcus Aurelius Antonius in the Capitol in Rome, the portrait of an individual and the representative of a type, is the first equestrian figure in Western art. The best of the Greek tradition is in it and the subtlety of Roman observation all combined with a superb craftsmanship.

The *Gattamelata* by Donatello and the *Colleoni* by Verrocchio, the masterpieces of the Renaissance, approach but cannot reach its serene harmony. Marcus Aurelius was a great emperor and a great philosopher whose Meditations are one of the major works of the Stoic school of thought. Both the figures of the man and the horse in this ancient monument express serenity and dignity to perfection. It was certainly the Chinese who in their grave figurines of the T'ang Dynasty gave

The Concept of the Rider. 1956. Polychrome wood. 78 ³/₄″ × 36 ¹/₄″ × 55 ⁷/₈″. Weintraub Gallery, New York.

Dancer. 1953. Polychrome plaster. 61″ × 12 ⁵/₈″ × 13 ⁷/₈″. Property of the artist.

form to the greatest variety of the states of the human soul in a perfect sculptural manner. It was certainly these classic examples of East and West which ignited the spark in Marini. He realized that the equestrian figure could be used as a symbol of modern man's joys and struggles, as a symbol of contemporary mankind. The creative idea behind it was to employ both the animal and the human form as vehicles of the same expression heightening the effect through the divergency of their shapes as well as through their capacity for experiencing similar emotions.

"To us Italians who are a political nation," so Marini said to me[3], "an equestrian figure gives a sensation of something heroic, romantic. This sensation changes all the time but it also remains always the same. Sometimes the horsemen are sad, sometimes they are gay, sometimes, again, tragic. The tragedy is completed when the man falls from his horse. This is the poetry of man and horse. All is quiet, peaceful. Suddenly the form starts to be agitated, it becomes sad, is riddled with anxiety, tragedy. And this throughout the ages; when the age is peaceful the horses become quiet, sweet, when it changes they become sad, unhappy."

Marini calls all his equestrian figures: Horseman or Horse and Rider, and leaves it to us to visualize the inner implications.

### A Scandal in England

One day, his love for horses and Northern women brought him into conflict with the police. For once and for a moment only he saw both in their perfection, alive not as a poet's dream—it was in London's Hyde Park and the police were English. Let us say, however, first that the main theme of Marini's entire work are man and horse, the juggler (another symbol of human struggle and endeavour), portraits, both of men and women—and nudes. The female form is the other great inspiration of Marini's, equalled only by his interest in the human head, the features of which allow him to penetrate deeply into the individuality of man, which is sacred to him, and the pure expression of man's mind. "I study the type, I wonder what goes on inside a head. The female form is a form of architecture, very closed (serré) sensual and human. The problems connected with it are always the same. It is like playing cards. The cards are always the same but the game is different. Everything begins and ends with women. Often I am more drawn to women than to anything else ..."

Speaking once of the North, he instantaneously connected it with the analytical spirit: "What we have to achieve is a balance (équilibre) of the head and the heart, between the intelligence and the sensibility. What always counts is the reserve of vitality and sensibility, only they can feed (donner la nutrition) the world. In our epoch we need more vitality, more life. There is blood in us,

Dancer. 1952/53. Bronze. Height: 61".
Baron Lambert Coll., Brussels.

Small Rider. 1950. Bronze. 11″ × 16 9/16″. Baronne Lambert Coll., Brussels.

warmth, there are smells. We Latins are sensual. We touch things, we taste them. And when representing something vital we must never leave out of sight the balance. They speak of modern art and tradition as if they were two different concepts. There is nothing new, but there is always a new approach—it depends on our fantasy."

Fantasy is a key word in Marini's artistic credo. "The same figure becomes another figure, a nude, which is not that of Donatello or Michelangelo or della Francesca, only thanks to our fantasy. We live now through a period of mechanization. Nevertheless, I like to ensure the presence of poetry (*J'aime assurer la poésie*). The poetry of today is our poetry. What is this period of ours about? Speed. This will end one day—a period is nothing when compared with eternity. Eternity, yes, there are things which belong to all periods." "The race has something to do with art. Henry Moore is a Northerner. The creators of the Gothic style were Northerners also. The North is always slightly abstract. Mediterranean man, on the other hand, is always sensual. Hence the need for equilibrium. Piero della Francesca is a Mediterranean. His art is not realism only, it is an art containing abstraction, but an abstraction which is human. The sun is decisive for us. We cannot neglect it. The flowers grow in the sun more richly, more colourfully. It is the sun which causes that. The artist also is animated by the sun. (*Les artistes sont poussés aussi.*) Now, you will ask, why are there Italian artists who follow the world trend of abstraction? I will answer you: The artists of today see too many illustrations from all countries. The danger in this is that it can become overwhelming. The risk is great. Every artist has to keep his soil, his face. Just as a flower which is born in a volcanic soil cannot live in another soil. The way of seeing things, of listening, is entirely different. But—when two phenomena meet there can be a surprise. If Moore descends here and I mount to the North—this would produce an "encounter" (*rencontre*), and the encounter might be felicitous. I, for instance, cannot work in the South—I was born near Florence, but it is the North which sets me in vibration. And the North seems always to tend towards the sun. I always search for the contrary of my nature and that is the North."

It was in 1929/30 when Marini visited London for the first time that he went one day to Hyde Park, to meet a friend. He was not very happy for he spoke no English and in the hotel at St. James's where he stayed nobody understood French. "I felt like a Negro. I made gestures all the time. One becomes mad here, I told myself. One cannot speak to anybody. I went up in the lift and I went down in the lift, dumb; I did not count, I was put aside. Naturally, I wanted to be the centre. I thought I had a chance in London. When I met my friend he was taking his morning ride between two ladies on horseback. A large party followed, more

Rider. 1951. Bronze. Height: 21 ⁵/₈". Joseph Hirshhorn Coll., Greenwich, USA.

young women, very refined, society women. They gathered, descended from their horses. I came to greet them. The combination of horse and woman, and such beautiful women of a classic type, Northern, aristocratic, blonde, made my head go round. They were as Dante Gabriel Rossetti used to paint women somehow, with a kind of complexion that is like a great tradition. I was a bit of a savage and these sophisticated girls were transparent— *claires comme la lune*. I love this skin. The veins, they can be traced. Here women are brown. I gazed at them as at the head of Medusa, and could not do otherwise than go forward and embrace

35

Horse. 1951. Bronze. 90 ⁵/₈″ × 82 ⁵/₈″. Museum of Contemporary Art of the University of Sao Paulo.

one of them. I approached the nearest one like a sleep-walker and kissed her. I had the impression of embracing the moon—*J'ai eu l'impression d'embrasser la lune.* There was a scene, police were called, my friend excused me, I apologized. There, you see: myself, the North, the attraction, the contrast."

(1) Gilbert Murray, *Five Stages of Greek-Religion*.
(2) Another time (1952) he quoted as his sources of inspiration: the Gothic, the Egyptian, the Greek, the Etruscan and the Pre-Columbian styles.
(3) Conversation in Venice, June, 1952.

# The Exhibition in Rome

## by Giovanni Carandente

No man is a prophet in his own country. Marino Marini proved no exception to that rule, at least until 1966 when he was officially crowned at the Capitol or, to be more precise, a stone's throw away from there, in the Palazzo Venezia that a cardinal of the Serene Republic had built in the fifteenth century to be his residence as well as that of the Muses. The exhibition that was held in the three large rooms of the Palace and on the ground floor (in an old room that was once affected to a religious order) consisted of drawings, paintings and sculptures from 1923 to 1965 and

was the first official show devoted to the artist in his own country. As the President of the Committee, Ercole Marazza, wrote in his preface to the catalog, Marini is not adequately represented in Italian public collections; on the other hand, he is one of the very rare artists who is justly included in major public and private collections in Europe and the United States.

Marino Marini was born at Pistoia and grew up in an atmosphere in which the artistic influences inherited from Giovanni Pisano and fra' Guglielmo could be felt. Although he assimilated all the

Miracle. 1959/60. Polychrome wood. About 70 $^7/_8$″ × 51 $^3/_{16}$″ × 114 $^3/_{16}$″. Galleria Civica d'Arte Moderna, Turin. *Exhibition at the Palazzo Venezia in Rome, 1966.*

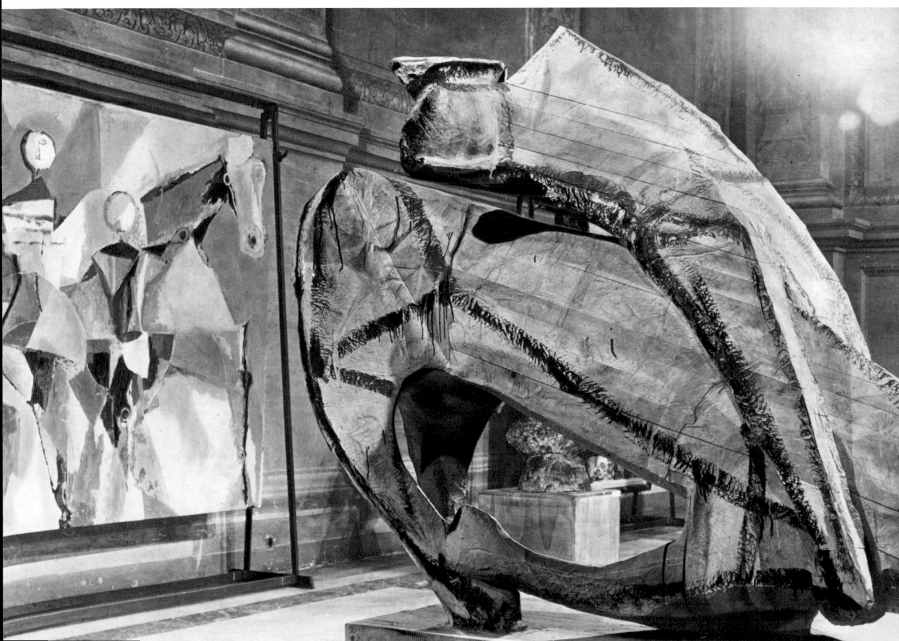

rhythms and accents of the modern language of art, he looked closely at the Etruscans and has always remained basically Tuscan just as Ghiberti and Donatello were in their time.

He was fourteen when he met Rodin in Florence. The author of the *Bourgeois de Calais* and the young Tuscan with his soft and timid features reminiscent of those of the young people one can see in the reliefs by Desidero da Settignano or by Rossellino, did not have time to talk much. It is said that the old sculptor and the young apprentice sat down next to each other on the stone balustrade that stretches in front of the wall around the convent of Saint Mark, close to the place where the gardens of Lawrence the Magnificent were located and where Michelangelo learned to model, and that they sat there a moment without speaking.

Marini was studying at the "Accademia"—the School of Fine Arts—in Florence, taking a course given by an academic sculptor who is more known today for his teaching than for his work. It was as a painter that Marini made his first efforts, and his painterly apprenticeship went hand in hand with an intense study and practice of drawing. His earliest work, which was on view at the exhibition, is a study of two female figures seen from the back; it is dated 1926 and already gives an idea of the way in which Marini would handle the problem of form. To be more precise, it shows a desperate attempt to reconquer a sense of form combined with a peremptory affirmation of the plastic substance and a keen and realistic interest in the female figure. All these traits would soon profoundly change the provincial climate of a country in which, with the exception of the rare archaic attempts by Modigliani, of a few dynamic experiments by Boccioni and of the distinguished but limited work of Arturo Martini, sculpture was only capable of producing chimney-piece ornaments or pompous and affected monuments.

So Marini began to draw and to paint dynamic, expanding forms based on the theme of woman, eternal matrix out of which all life springs. These he then transposed into sculpture in order to more fully stress, underline and embody the form. The great masters before him, Renoir, Maillol as well as Bourdelle, Despiau and Laurens, had proceeded in a similar way. But the problem as Marini saw it required different solutions than those, so varied among themselves but equally vital, of the French sculptors. There was another factor: the discovery of Picasso's work opened up a new path for Marini, showing how it was possible both to distort and at the same time to reconstruct form. Marini also saw a way in which a formal rigor might be achieved that would be different from that defended by the sculptors who adopted the new plastic reality without abandoning an original archaism.

Marini was not yet thirty when he began to carve in hard pear tree wood the sculpture entitled *Ersilia* which today can be seen at the Kunsthaus in Zurich. He infused this earthly idol, made of petrified flesh and full of a magic sensual energy, with the new rhythm of a sculptural style as well as with an hallucinatory truth.

Marini came to Paris for the first time in 1928, and the lessons of those who were in the forefront of the avant-garde did not go unheeded. He met Gonzalez and Kandinsky, Braque and Picasso. But how could he forget the dried up situation of Italian art in those years? This constant reminder determined the path his work would follow.

Certainly Marini did not start from zero. However, his starting point was neither the Hellenism of Maillol nor the mysterious world of the ceramic T'ang figurines. Both the former and the latter as cultural references formed part of a repertory of basic images that he used later in order to affirm a new form that was neither figurative nor symbolic but evoked rather the most intact image that the figure was capable of conserving after the powerful impact of Cubism.

In 1929 Marini put his stamp on an unusual terracotta sculpture, *The People*. This work shows a frank and popular sense of humor that has its antecedents in the Etruscan urns of Volterra; it is both natural and symbolic, linking together the characteristics and presences of the form with the realistic contents and the skillful and sensitive exposure of the plastic surfaces to the light.

Marini continued to build up his repertory as if he were exploring unknown lands for themes: portraits, swimmers, wrestlers, adolescents. These were the first anticipations of a vocabulary of figures that later assumed the most rigorous coherence. It was a truly unique experience to see all the marvelous *Pomonas* reunited together at the exhibition in Rome, from the first (1941) which belongs to the Jesi collection in Milan to the last (1949) from the Wilhelm Lehmbruck Museum in Duisburg which has such a refined, opulent sense of color. To give a more precise idea of the experience, think of what it would be like to see all of De Kooning's *Women* brought together in one place. The great, imposing figures of these earth goddesses, of these non-symbolic symbols of truth and fertility, these mythic creatures which seem bound to the earth as a tree is to its roots, dominated the sadly famous Salon de la Mappemonde, finally redeeming the Mussolinian rhetoric that had domiciled itself there for twenty years. At the time, when Marini had exhibited his first attempts on the theme of horse and rider, his bare, *non-heroic* groups had only aroused the laughter of the critics.

Although it might seem strange, Marini's equestrian theme was not inspired by the remembrance of the plastic myths of the Renaissance, the statues of horses and condottieri. In the back of his creative consciousness he curiously united the myth of the Roman group of Marcus Aurelius and the nordic horsemen, such as *Henry the II* of the Bamberg Cathedral, giving more importance to the latter than to the former, more importance to the gothic than to the measured elegance of the

Dancer. 1949. Bronze.
Height: 46 1/16".
W. and N. Bär Coll.,
Zurich.
*Exhibition
the Palazzo Venezia
in Rome, 1966.*

In the foreground: Rider. 1936. Bronze. 63″ × 80 ³/₄″. Emilio Jesi Coll., Milan. In the center: Gentleman on a Horse. 1937. Bronze. Height: 61 ³/₈″. Camera dei Deputati, Rome. On the left: The Pilgrim 1939. Bronze. Height: 68 ¹/₈″ × 16 ⁹/₁₆″ × 48 ⁷/₈″. Emilio Jesi Coll., Milan. *Exhibition at the Palazzo Venezia in Rome, 1966. (Photos Bo Boustedt).*

Renaissance. This preference finally kept Marini from falling into the domain of archeology, be it that of the Far East, of the Far West or of Renaissance Tuscany.

Marini is fond of saying that out of a need for renewal he passed from the formal vigor of his soil to the cold visions of the North and in this way found his identity as a European sculptor. This is quite true. The 1946 equestrian couple reveals a new treatment of volume and space as well as a new relationship between horse and rider. A tension is established between the two forces that will increase constantly. Sometimes the horse rises vigorously, as if ready to leap, dominating space, or is stretched out in an energetic movement full of sensuality; sometimes the rider falls backward on its hindquarters and becomes one with the mass of the animal.

Marini's fidelity to the horse and rider motif gave him the same gamut of incessant variations as the *Reclining Figure* did to Henry Moore. The sculptor brought all the resources of matter into play. He shook out forms in space as if they were the desperate, tattered strips of a humanity relentlessly declining everywhere except on an intellectual level. He intensified the relationship of power, going so far as to destroy it in order to transform it into one lonely cry in space. And never did he show any literary complacency in this dereliction of the myth of man, save, perhaps, in the titles of his works. To his last work he gave an abstract title, *Composition of Elements*, thus removing the literary ingredient that was only a result of the apogee which figuration had reached.

Assembled in the two large rooms of the Palazzo Venezia, the great horses and riders from the second period of the artists unfolded before the spectator a steady progression of creative tension and infused him with that feeling of coherence and authenticity that is the mark of a Master.

*From XXᵉ siècle, no. 28, Paris 1967.*

In the center: Pomona. 1949. Bronze. Height: 66 ¹/₈″. Statens Museum for Kunst, Copenhagen. On the right: Pomona. 1945. Stone. Height: 68 ⁷/₈″. W. and N. Bär Coll., Zurich. *Exhibition at the Palazzo Venezia in Rome, 1966.*

41

# Marino Marini at the Villa Reale in Milan

## AN EXEMPLARY DONATION

*by Lara-Vinca Masini*

The *Portraits* (generally of famous and important people) have a special place in the work of Marino Marini. They constitute in a way the synthesis of his researches into the formal means of expression and show how a subtle and attentive eye has re-examined the plastic achievements of every epoch. Stretching over a rather long period of the artist's activity, they parallel the other works in which Marini's style and trademark are unmistakably clear (*Pomonas, Warriors, Horses*). In short, they might be considered as a very particular, almost psychosomatic analysis that permitted the artist to verify his formal and cultural autonomous expressive necessities. Hence the extreme importance of this part of the artist's work.

Marino Marini has recently donated the *Portraits* belonging to him as well as the preparatory drawings that accompany them to the Museum of Modern Art in Milan. This donation consists of thirty-three pieces in terracotta, polychrome plaster and bronze dating from 1929 to 1967. A few other major works that belong to the wife of the artist, Marina Marini, have also been given on loan: a bronze *Pomona* of 1941, a *Horse* of 1953, also in bronze, a series of small *Jugglers* and *Acrobats*, about twenty small bronzes and terracottas, a few well-known pictures (*Giselle*, 1923; *The Algerian Woman*, 1927; *The Carriage Builder's Daughters*, 1957, etc.), as well as an important group of lithographs, watercolors and aquatints from different periods (many examples of the ar-

A room containing part of the Marini donation to the Galleria Civica d'Arte Moderna. From left to right: Henry Moore (1962), Juggler (1932), Giuditta Campigli (1943), Stravinsky (1951), Nelson Rockefeller (1950), Jean Arp (1963) and De Pisis (1941).

In the foreground: Pomona. 1941. Bronze. Height: 63". In the background: The Carriage Builder's Daughters. 1957. Oil on canvas. 59" × 59". Loaned by Marina Marini to the Galleria Civica d'Arte Moderna, Milan. (*Photos Ancillotti*).

tist's graphic work are already in the museum's collection).

This donation is exemplary for more than one reason. First of all, the artist has given a public organization an important part of his work, thus withdrawing it from commerce. The response of the museum was commensurate with the gift and showed that it was aware of the value of Marino Marini's gesture: six rooms of the Villa Reale on via Palestro were set aside for the donation (other collections and donations—Della Ragione and so many others—are dispersed among different reserves in Florence still waiting to be brought together in a hypothetical museum of contemporary art. In this respect, what is happening to the "Marino Marini" Museum in Florence that has been talked about so much? It is satisfying to see that the event in Milan has revived an interest in and has updated this project).

The way the six rooms at the Villa Reale have been equipped is also exemplary. At the request of Marino himself, a specialist in optical and perceptual problems was commissioned to do the work; he is also a painter, a sculptor and the author of fantastic architectural drawings whose pseudonym, Arcturus, conceals a man who refuses any personal compromise. Founder of the Centro Studi Piero della Francesca, he has devoted his life to safeguarding and restoring our sculptural patrimony, whether this involves preserving works that have been exposed to atmospheric degradations or putting on a proper critical level those that have been abandoned to the arbitrary tastes of the market and of private collectors and hence do not yet belong to the collective cultural patrimony. In this context the large exhibitions of ancient sculpture organized by Arcturus in Milan (the Abbey of Chiaravallo), in Venice (San Salvatore), in Bergamo, etc., will be recalled.

In 1972 the Centro Studi Piero della Francesca organized in its headquarters on via Montenapoleone in Milan an exhibition of *Portraits* by Marino Marini. The presentation of this exhibit was so carefully thought out that Marino decided to call on its organizer for the installation of the rooms at the Villa Reale.

Six rooms were thus put aside to receive the donation. In the first the graphic work may be

Foreground: Horse and Rider. 1955. Bronze. 88 $^9/_{16}$″ × 35 $^7/_{16}$″ × 55 $^7/_8$″. On the left: Stage Set. 1960. Oil on canvas. 77 $^{15}/_{16}$″ × 66 $^1/_8$″. On the right: Rider, study. 1951. Bronze. 10 $^3/_8$″ × 11 $^5/_8$″ × 71 $^1/_2$″. Loaned by Marina Marini to the Galleria Civica d'Arte Moderna, Milan. (*Photo Ancillotti*).

seen; in the second the small "theater" of the *Jugglers* and *Acrobats*; the *Portraits* are grouped in a third room, as are the preparatory drawings in the fourth where an automatic slide projector makes it possible to see the whole group of *Portraits*; the large *Pomona* and the *Horse* stand respectively in the last two rooms. There was obviously no intention of modifying in any way the inner arrangement of the Villa Reale, which was built in the eighteenth century and whose monumental size is badly adapted to modern museographical installations. Insofar as possible, then, an effort was made to separate "form" and "contents" by means of panels suspended from the beams and the railings on the ceilings. These were painted dark gray (except for those in the room of the *Portraits*, where the original frescoes were kept), and a few white bands on them reflect the light. The most interesting novelty is precisely the indirect lighting provided by the spotlights hidden on the inside of the upper part of the beams; they project the light on the white bands on the ceiling from where it is reflected, depending on the angles and the distances, into the rooms, thus

creating special angles of vision. The sculptures are in this way bathed by a succession of shadow and light. On the other hand, a uniform lighting was given to the paintings and the graphic works, some of which (the color lithographs) are further illumined by a light attached to the inside of their frame. This creates an unusual and very stimulating visual effect. In the rooms where the *Pomona* and the *Horse* are on view, there is a mobile lighting system that consists of mirrors that can turn freely upon which luminous beams are alternately projected.

But by far the most spectacular effect belongs to the room that contains the small "theater" of the ten *Jugglers* and *Acrobats*. A veritable ballet of light, carefully adjusted and made even more dynamic by the particular movements of the light sources and by the alternation of light and shadow, gives them a truly astonishing presence.

Hopefully initiatives of this kind will not remain isolated and unique occurrences but will encourage the museums and public institutions to adopt a more positive and responsible attitude toward the art of our time.

The Idea of an Image, 1969/70. Bronze. Height: about 196 $\frac{1}{8}$". (*Courtyard of the Villa Reale in Milan*).

Part of the Marino Marini Donation to the Galleria Civica d'Arte Moderna of Milan. From left to right: Portrait of Marc Chagall, 1962, polychrome plaster, height: 11 3/4". Juggler, 1932, polychrome plaster, height: 67 5/16". Portrait of Giuditta Campigli, 1943, polychrome plaster, height: 12 5/8".

Works loaned by Marina Marini to the Galleria Civica d'Arte Moderna of Milan. From left to right: Characters in a Circus II, 1949. Mixed media, 36 1/4" × 28 3/8". Jugglers, 1955, oil on canvas, 31 1/2" × 25 5/8". Yellow and Blue, 1951, tempera, paper mounted on canvas, 37 3/8" × 26 13/16".

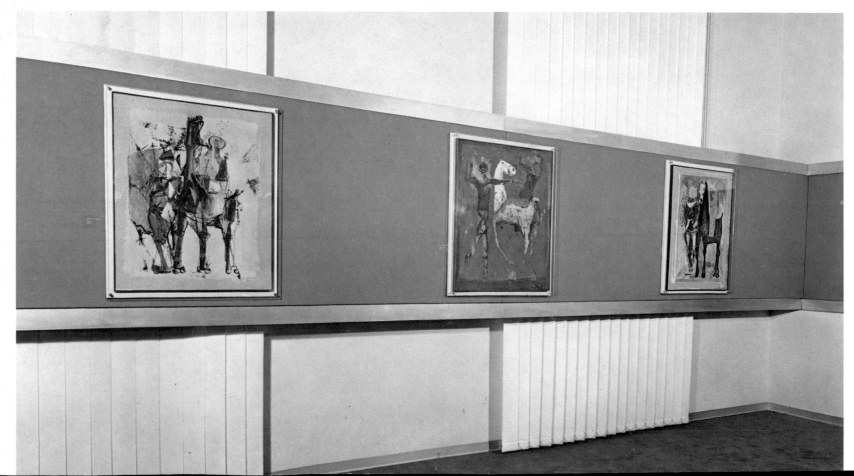

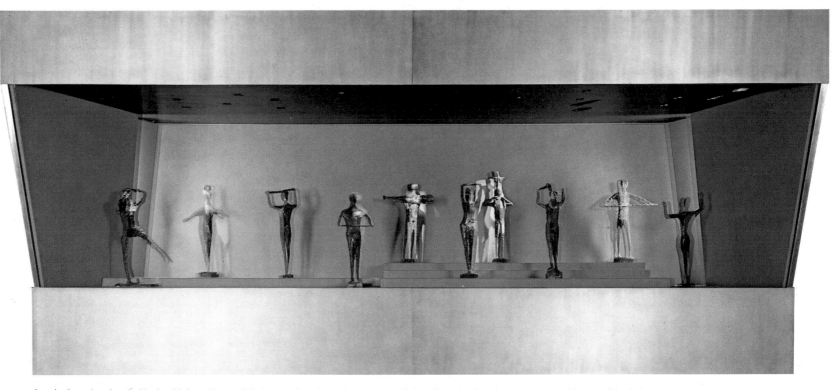

A window in the Galleria Civica d'Arte Moderna showing the ten small jugglers in bronze loaned by Marina Marini.

Detail of the window.

# TRUER THAN TRUTH

## by Raffaele Carrieri

Between January and April, 1972, the *Portraits* that Marino Marini has just donated to the city of Milan were exhibited at the "Centro Studi Piero della Francesca" under the title *Personages of the 20th Century.*

In truth, the title given to this exhibition was rather generic as I did not see any "personages." But with respect to the art of the portrait, I doubt if the quality of the thirty sculptures that were on view at the Villa Reale has been equalled in our time. Some of these portraits have travelled more times around the world than they have been exhibited, in particular those of Stravinsky, Nelson Rockefeller, Curt Valentin, Emma Jeker, Arcangelo, Henry Moore, Marina, Emilio Jesi, Germaine Richier, Campigli, Carlo Carrà, De Pisis. It seems to me that this was the first time in Italy that so many portraits by Marino were exhibited together. From the terracotta *The Bourgeoise* which dates from 1928 to the bronze of Mies Van der Rohe which was completed in 1967, a marvelous anthology of men and women brought to life by an extraordinary creative power could be seen.

I had not seen the busts of the couple in *The People* (1929) for a long time. How is it possible not to think of the Etruscans or of Baudelaire's phrase, "Sculpture is brutal and positive like nature"? Part of this brutality is evident in *The People*, but it is subordinated to vision, to the pressure that form exerts on characters and to the harshness with which these characters have been stamped. A close inspection reveals that this harshness has to do more with "grammar" than with real contents. It is an expression of the desire to bring forms and characters together by means of masses. This attempt is repeated in *The Bourgeoise* but on a reduced scale and with a form that is more supple. As if out of reaction, harshness yields to affability. As for the masses, far from being inert, they stand at the very source of the rhythm which they determine thanks to the assemblage of planes in a firm and concise plastic structure. The characters control the cadence and form is imparted by constructive values. After 1933, Marino's sculpture grew more schematic, nervous, and acquired fullness, concentration and subtlety. The thicknesses, the contours that were too heavy, and the slightly static chiaroscuro of certain old allegories disappeared. The formal structure was purified, became more fluid and at the same time was charged with an extreme tension. The lines by themselves alone were capable of expressing the entire contents. There was no archaic spirit.

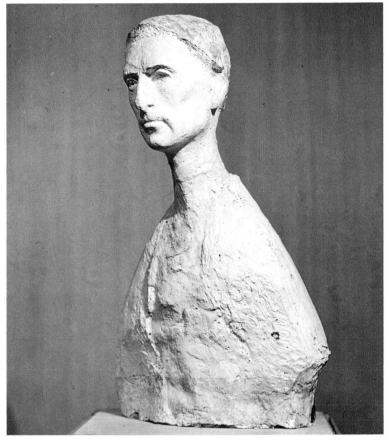

Archangel. 1943. Polychrome plaster. Height: 27 ⁹/₁₆″. Galleria Civica d'Arte Moderna, Milan.

Portrait of Massimo Campigli. 1942. Bronze. Height: 15″. Galleria Civica d'Arte Moderna, Milan.

◁ Portrait of Emma Jeker. 1947. Polychrome plaster. Height: 13 ³/₄″. Galleria Civica d'Arte Moderna, Milan.

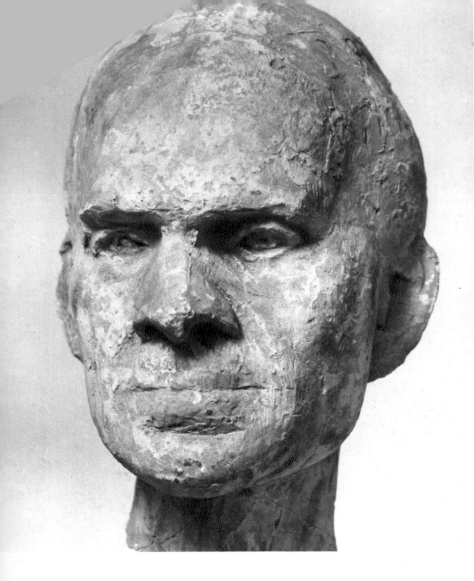

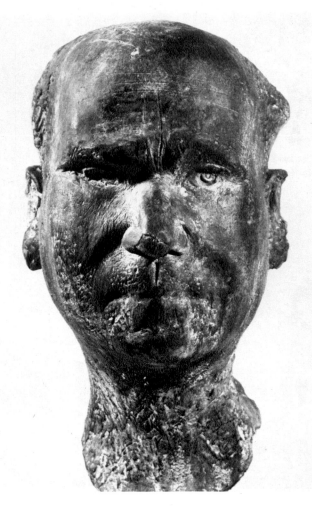

Portrait of Riccardo Jucker. 1950. Polychrome plaster. Height: 14 ³/₁₆″. Galleria Civica d'Arte Moderna, Milan.

◁ Portrait of Henry Miller. Detail. 1961. Plaster. Height: 10 ¹³/₁₆″. Galleria Civica d'Arte Moderna, Milan.

Portrait of Filippo De Pisis. 1941. Bronze. Height: 13 ³/₄″. Galleria Civica d'Arte Moderna, Milan.

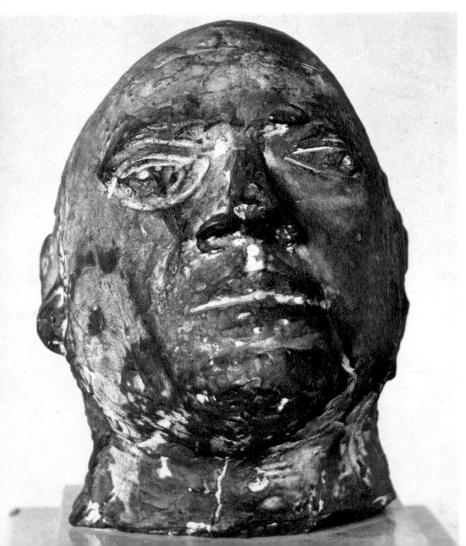

The portraits, whose dates of execution vary so much, all bear witness to the same stylistic unity. The plaster of Angelo Lanza (1928) has the same freshness and power as the polychrome plaster of Carl Georg Heise which was done thirty-four years later. The same holds true for the superb, sensitive portrait in polychrome plaster of Marc Chagall (1962). The bronze of Campigli (1942) and that of Filippo De Pisis (1941) are finished masterpieces. The same can be said for the portrait of Igor Stravinsky (1951) and that of Henry Miller (1961).

Marino lives inside his forms. He enters into the clay, and the clay ceases to be a material of simple potency. It is like the secret of a twin birth. It is not a question of progressing, of going further ahead, of developing consciousness or showing knowledge. It is not a question of doing better. Or of understanding. Or of making oneself understood. What is at stake is rather a transformation of each thing into a single substance that is at one and the same time universal and personal. It is rediscovering the center and the rhythm: the continuity. It is liberating oneself from the body and the servitudes of repetition. It is beginning again, from form to form, similar to God during the first days of Creation.

Portrait of Curt Valentin. 1954. Bronze. Height: 9 ¹/₄″. Galleria Civica d'Arte Moderna, Milan.

# SMALL AND LARGE SCULPTURES

## by A.M. Hammacher

When I saw again the nine *Small Jugglers* of 1951-1953 at the Galleria d'Arte Moderna in Milan, where they are exhibited with much taste and sensibility in a small museum that groups together a selection of Marino Marini's works, I found myself closer to the artist's creative source than I had ever been before. For years the group of *Small Jugglers* had stood on the mantelpiece in the living room of Marini's apartment on the Piazza Mirabello in Milan. In the intimacy of this environment it was possible to see a certain identity between their expressions and movements and those of the artist. The total effect they produced was so direct, powerful and definitive that one simply forgot their small size. In the museum they had neighbors: other small sculptures like those plaster torsos or polychrome terracottas of 1929, the voluptuous and seductive *Seated Venus* in polychrome terracotta of 1929-30 which is no higher than seven inches, the bronze 1932 *Juggler* and the *Small Juggler* of 1956 which looks eaten by sickness or some ineffaceable corrosion. There were also some very small bronzes (2 ½″ to 4 ½″ high) called "studies," and that served as the preliminary ideas for sculptures which were executed later or perhaps even abandoned. There were, then, small sculptures that were sketches and others that, as they were complete even in their small size, did not demand to be enlarged.

The feeling of space that one admires in the

From left to right: Small Boxer, 1935, bronze, 7 $^{11}/_{16}$″ × 3 $^{1}/_{8}$″ × 5 $^{1}/_{8}$″. Small Miracle, 1955, bronze, 9 $^{3}/_{16}$″ × 6 $^{11}/_{16}$″. Small Seated Venus, 1929/30, polychrome terracotta, height: 7 $^{1}/_{8}$″. Dancer, 1929, polychrome terracotta, height: 11″. Small Nude, 1929, polychrome plaster, height: 7 $^{1}/_{2}$″. Juggler, 1932, bronze, 10 $^{3}/_{4}$″ × 3 $^{1}/_{8}$″ × 3 $^{1}/_{8}$″. Loaned by Marina Marini to the Galleria Civica d'Arte Moderna, Milan. (*Photo Ancillotti*).

From left to right: Small Pomona, 1943, bronze, height: 17 ¹/₁₆″. Small Pomona, 1943, bronze, height: 16 ³/₈″. Small Pomona, 1943, bronze, height: 16 ⁵/₈″. Loaned by Marina Marini to the Galleria Civica d'Arte Moderna, Milan. (*Photo Ancillotti*).

room of the large *Pomona* as well as in that of the *Horse and Rider* with its vehement verticality, bears no relationship to that evoked by the small sculptures, and yet one cannot explain this simply by the difference in scale. The large sculptures are conditioned by their environment, for instance, by the rhythm of the landscape in which they are located or their position inside or outside of an architectural ensemble. Contrary to these great silent volumes, the small sculptures continue to live even if one picks them up. Marini's sense of proportion and his sensibility are well-known. In

the *Portraits* he never enlarges the face of his model and an imperceptible diminution of the volumes in relation to reality can even be observed. Most of the time these *Portraits* are no higher than twelve inches, for example, that of Carlo Carrà (9 ½″), of Fausto Melotti (head 12″, bust 14 ½″), of Emilio Jesi (9 ½″), of the Baroness Treves (8″). Undoubtedly the extraordinary concentration of the artist, reading and interpreting the face of his models, is responsible for the slight diminution of the volumes.

What happened with respect to the *Jugglers* in

1951-53 is even more significant. The artist had been working on this theme for a long time. It suffices to look at the *Juggler* of 1932 to see that it is closer to the series of *Jugglers* of 1950-53 than to that of 1939. The latter, however, is the most naturalistic; its forms are round, heavy, full of sap—just as Marini loves them to be—and they can be traced back to prehistoric art and those women, symbols of fertility, whose breasts, bellies and thighs are heavily accentuated. Moreover, the three small *Pomonas* of 1943 are the modern sisters of the Venus of Willendorf.

After 1940, the depiction of erotico-plastic elements became more restrained in the artist's work. The forms of the *Dancers* of the fifties are less full and more stylized, although the body is still highly structured and stands out melodiously in the surrounding space. During that period Marini sculpted with a greater economy of means and his works became thinner and more svelte. But although, starting in the fifties, this tendency was accentuated and sometimes dominated his output, it would be a mistake to think that it was caused by contempt for the body or for sensuality. The happy psychic identification of the artist with the theme of acrobats and jugglers created a mental image that existed in a state of dangerous equilibrium but was controlled by a supreme mastery of body and spirit.

Marini has always loved the world of the circus. There is a film in which he can be seen in the company of acrobats, clowns and jugglers, and their mutual behavior testifies to deep emotion and moving respect. His relationship with the circus should not just be thought of as the dying echo of a romanticism that is now a little outmoded. Watteau, Seurat, Picasso and Rouault come to mind for they all loved to portray this eternal theme that is even represented—full of music with its instruments, voices and games—in certain medieval sculptures as well as in the mural paintings of Pompeii. Later this light, musical ambiance was adopted by the troubadours and jugglers. Marini's *Jugglers*, *Acrobats* and *Horses*, which can be seen at the Galleria d'Arte Moderna, have a surprising formal simplicity that conceals a complex and unique perception of space.

In addition to these small "studies" that were preparatory works for the large sculptures, there are, as I have mentioned, many other small sculptures that belong more particularly to the artist's intimate conception of space. However, a close look at them reveals that all these *Small Jugglers* and small *Pomonas* possess their own reality and sense of space, regardless of whether they stand in a museum, in a city or a landscape. These small-scale works have no ambition to be anything but what they are, to form part of a world that was created to be seen and therefore read. Small or large, their size does not have and should not have any importance. This whole interpretation

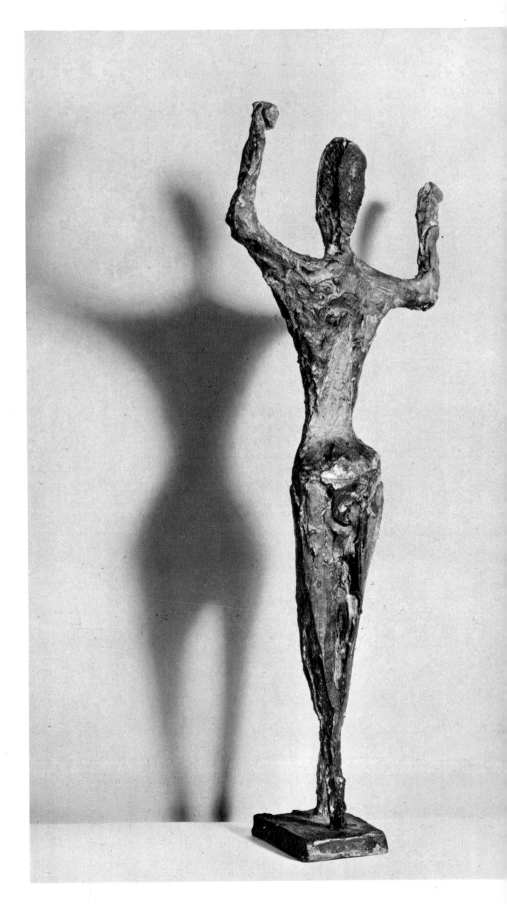

Small Juggler. 1953. Polychrome bronze. Height: 18 15/16". Loaned by Marina Marini to the Galleria Civica d'Arte Moderna, Milan.

of space is not yet ready to be measured nor is it yet entirely subordinated to the stable norms of reason. There is an intellectual and sensual pleasure in finding that many of these sculptures are nothing but the extension of Marini's hands and fingers. They are both a testimony enabling the viewer to participate in the creation of a world in space and in the life that the artist has infused matter with. They emerge from the images born inside all the dreams, impressions, sensations and thoughts of the sculptor. In order to be sure of surviving, they must conquer the hesitations, natural aversions and fears of leaving such a warm shelter to confront the hostility of the real world. At last the artist's creative process can be understood, the efforts that he must make to crystallize his images that go from the world of his dreams to the world of reality in which, occasionally, they originate. When I stand in front of them, the small sculptures always make me feel closer to the creative sources of the sculptor than the large ones do.

The *Jugglers* of the fifties announced the definitive appearance in Marino Marini's work of a thin, svelte, threadlike sculpture that was neither abstract nor bruised in its substance but modelled in a precise, geometrical spirit which never impedes the flow of life's vibrations. In spite of their lack of relief, the figurines are endowed with a minimal thickness that is revealed when they are seen in profile and especially when they revolve, as they do at the Galleria d'Arte Moderna. These thin, svelte figures have an historical background which is not confined only to Etruscan art. Other artists come to mind, such as Donatello, Giacometti, Picasso, Gonzalez (not to mention abstract sculptors), and especially Germaine Richier and the corroded, dark, upsetting and even terrifying matter of her sculptures, in particular those of the fifties. Marini met her in Switzerland during the war. Although certain resemblances might be seen between them, Marini obviously does not share Germaine's fondness for whatever is macabre, hallucinatory, hybrid, nor her very personal dynamism.

I have still said nothing about the color painted on the *Small Jugglers*. Color plays an important role in Marini's sculpture. It seems to have its own life and yet does not always take into account the rationality of the proportions and of the anatomy of the figures. And yet these stains, reddish like wine lees or dark blue, these golden scratches on the surface of the bronze, could not be more in their place. On the very surface of the sculpture lines of color and forms flower, flow together and merge; there is nothing extraneous.

By means of his colored, nervous graphism and his balanced forms, Marini reinforced and intensified his contact with that mysterious world suspended between the inner and the outer, that world of transcendence, of living transformation that is but metamorphosis.

# Sculptures in the City

## by Pierre Volboudt

The city can be thought of as an abstract theater designed for anonymous and disparate activities; nature is only accepted in it to the degree to which it is subordinated to the city's order and structure, by which it is enclosed. Man also uses the city as a way of defending himself against these natural forces that attack him and of keeping them at a distance. The stage set of the city, to continue the metaphor, is made up of countless buildings and perspectives that were put there for the use, convenience or entertainment of man. The statues that man erects are immobile actors in a perpetual improvisation, the unwilling accomplices of all the too empty squares, the monumental reply to the passers-by who move by their feet, avoid them and, distracted, look at them without seeing them. Stylized and natural representations are themselves only admitted into the city as objects whose sole function is to fill some gap in the urban environment. Quincunxes of columns, rocks turned into pedestals, bronze horses, petrified heroic walkons, and legendary fauna, are all adapted to the pure equilibriums of which man makes his dwelling, divided between the pomp of geometry and the servitude of everyday needs. If the space necessary for its development is threatened, the city

From left to right: Female Statuette, study, 1954, bronze, $3\,^1/_8''\times 1\,^9/_{16}''\times 1\,^3/_8''$. Reclining Woman, study, 1954, bronze, $1\,^5/_8''\times 4''\times 1\,^9/_{16}''$. Small Miracle, 1970, bronze, $5\,^7/_{16}''\times 1\,^9/_{16}''\times 1\,^3/_8''$. Female Statuette, study, 1954, bronze, height: $4\,^3/_8''$. Female Statuette, study, 1954, bronze, $2\,^{15}/_{16}''\times 1\,^9/_{16}''\times 1\,^9/_{16}''$. Small Composition, 1956, bronze, $5\,^3/_8''\times 4\,^1/_2''\times 4\,^3/_8''$. Small Pomona, 1950, bronze, height: $5\,^3/_{16}''$. Composition, study, 1956, bronze, $6\,^{15}/_{16}''\times 4\,^3/_4''\times 3\,^3/_8''$. Loaned by Marina Marini to the Galleria Civica d'Arte Moderna, Milan. (*Photo Ancillotti*).

simply mobilizes its massive structures, lines up its concrete cliffs, drives broad estuaries through them, open everywhere to the flow of traffic. Around these enormous warehouses of humanity, an unending migration has only a need for reference points, arrows, panels. What do these vain witnesses of its flux and reflux mean to the city? Their images are as anachronistic as that of a horse stamping on its pedestal, as an allegory in its niche.

Individual man is absent from these metropolises. He has been lost in the crowd. It is no longer he who wanders in the street, stopping and going, endlessly passing by, but an infinitely fragmented version of Everyman. This character only pays attention to distances, routes, traffic lights and the super highways where he gets lost and grows impatient. Faceless, he has no contact with

The Angel of the City. 1949. Bronze. Height: 70⅞". Peggy Guggenheim Coll., Venice.

himself any more than he has with nature, about which he cares nothing. The only thing that interests him are his own agitations and the temporary relief given by his manipulated excitements.

The age in which statuary was associated with architecture clearly belongs to the past. Our age of enormous volumes, sprawling space, masses and quantitative numbers seems better suited to elementary images and powerful, bony structures in which the shapeless, inert but potentially energetic forms of nature slumber. The artist can act as mediator between these two different orders of reality: the first is the deliberate one that the builder constructs with the help of machines whose functioning reduces men to the level of atoms; the second has to do with the violent forces that are at work in nature. The builder, in the last analysis, accentuates the aforementioned problems of the city; his buildings, for example, only create more promiscuity and add an extravagant, abstract design which towers above the crisscrossing lines of the traffic. It is the artist's job to introduce permanently into this something of the savage and disordered genius of universal tectonics in all its original roughness.

The art of Marino Marini, by virtue of its intense realism which seems to have weathered all the storms of a millenary evolution, is in accord with the rough facts of the world's substance such as they have been patiently shaped by chance and time. Out of that comes the sculptor's vision—an obsession—of his human figures that have been stripped and simplified down to the inevitable framework of mineral creation. The strict formulas of the engineer, when they are materialized in space, serve to underline the paradoxical affinity of Marini's forms not only with the rugged plasticity of nature's spontaneous creations but also with the arbitrary bareness of numbers and the symmetry of mathematical equations. They are as much related to the former as they challenge the latter, into which they nonetheless introduce— calculated dissonance or instinctive complicity— the complementary structures of their clear and vigorous essence.

At its final degree of achievement, sculpture for Marini becomes an exercise in rigor, a tragic architecture. His concern, as he himself puts it, is to attain a form that is as far removed from the human figure as it approximates a "constructive and static" line. Although the theme disintegrates into concrete and organic unreality, it is founded on reality which it re-creates by means of combinations of interlocking volumes in such a way that the first allusion is not basically modified.

The artist's chisel, however, keeps these virtual variations equidistant from all the appearances that a raw, untouched fragment might suggest. This is true for all the stages of the process, from the first sketch when the absolute form begins to emerge out of an incalculable series of chances and accidents to the final perfection when the hand has refined the contours and modelled the

Rider. 1951. Bronze. Height: About 45 ¼″. Manufacturers Hanover, New York.

without resistance. But this image grows more refined. The neck stretches out; the thin legs with the rounded fetlocks stiffen obliquely. A pyramidal composition takes shape that is completed by the man's head, which is rigid and ready to fall, while, on the contrary, the horse's forehead and neck are elongated horizontally. It is no longer so much a horse as a half fabulous animal that looks as if it is being torn apart in different directions.

A disequilibrium that is violently counterbalanced exists between the opposing tensions of the horse and rider. The diagonal, increasingly bent and lowered, that the latter forms is answered by the stretched, stiff line of the former, the interminable muzzle that is scarcely divided by the mouth and the flat rim of the nostrils. Although the rider is not yet unseated, he is now only the useless counterweight of the exaggerated elongation of the animal that sniffs some mysterious menace—one of those cataclysms at whose approach, terrified, it whinnies to the sky for help as its hooves scramble for a firm footing on the ground that already opens up and gives way.

The artist has never really explained his fondness for the recurrent attitude of the horse drawn back on its hocks as if shying away from some

◁ Equestrian Composition. 1957/58. Bronze.
Height: 177′8″. Monument at The Hague.

invisible obstacle. The triangular creature that it forms with its rider is, for the artist, the image of a desperate attempt to take root, the image as well of an impossible flight, and of straining flesh that cries out at the height of its efforts and is itself a cry.

The exaggerated deformations given by his hands to what they model led Marini to schematize the angular silhouette without any complacency. This form broadens out in trapezoids, its cohesion is broken and it is subordinated to the imperatives of a hard, violent geometry. The rider hangs on his mount like a derisory mannikin. Brute, animal strength is triumphant. This strength has something demoniacal about it and rises out of the depths of time, evoking images of herds and hordes. In the place of fallen man who can only be recognized by his gasp of agony, it gives voice to its shrill and silent plaint. Collapsing on its hindquarters, its eyes dilated, the horse vents its fury in one burst as it frantically struggles to tear itself out of the original chaos into which it is sinking. An art that seeks the "miracle"—if we may permit ourselves the use of a title that the artist has remained evasive about—finds here its most absolute expression. Does not all of Marini's work consist in uniting the harsh forms of the elementary with the plastic rigor that molds them in the shape of the idea?

After this excess and paroxysm, the passion shown in Marini's treatment of his materials grows calm. The great panic fever ebbs. The compact on which man founded his supremacy, which is forever vanquished and restored, becomes operative again. But this time he intends to surmount his defeat by associating himself with his adversary and partner; in other words, by joining up with those forces that caused his downfall. *Warrior*, if one likes, but rather a consenting victim, the protagonist of a fight with never-ending ups and downs in which he is pitted against inhuman powers that are now allies, now enemies, with whom he must constantly struggle for pre-eminence. The despotic rider of the past is super-

Warrior. 1959/60. Bronze. 53 $^1\!/_8$" × 66 $^{15}\!/_{16}$" × 44 $^7\!/_8$". Private Coll., Milan.

In the foreground: Small Miracle (rear view), 1972. On the right: The Concept of the Miracle. 1971. In the background: Ideal Composition. 1971. *International Open-Air Sculpture Exhibition, Rimini, 1971. (Photo Moretti film).*

ceded by this wild machine whose looks and behavior he must adopt as his own.

Here, the sculptor's path leads him into a dionysiac revery, into an imaginary anticipation of the future. Disjointed volumes are blended together and man and beast are merged into an enigmatic creature that squats and jealously guards the treasure of its forces. Marino Marini is pleased to have destroyed a myth. Has he not, on the contrary, helped to illustrate another myth that is even more disturbing than the one which was invented by the meanderings of the poetic imagination? Man believed that he had, once and for all, asserted his supremacy over all the things in the world. But their violence, which he thought he had tamed and domesticated, rebelled and took possession of him again. In front of the equivocal sphinx that the artist carved in dark stone, it is impossible to say where the animal ends and where man begins, and if, with respect to the

monster born of the mating of the distress of the former with the fury of the latter, the humiliation does not lie on the side of the one who pretended to have overthrown the balance of power in his favor.

Such a sculpture makes the viewer ask questions, makes him grow conscious of what, from one moment to another, can rise up and disturb the established order of things and demolish their fragile foundations. What the Greeks called by the name of hubris carries destruction in its wake and generates myths. The sculptor, willingly or not, contributes to this enterprise. Marino Marini participates in it. When the ground has at last been cleared and the architect begins to set up his forms and to organize them in space, Marino Marini makes manifest, in unusual contrasts, the protean form, the multiform reality that survives all destructions and constantly breaks through the surface of the new.

64

# The End of a Myth

## THE "MIRACLES"

*by Kurt Martin*

As if struck by some greater force, the powerful horse suddenly falls forward. The rider is thrown back onto the animal's hindquarters. His position makes it look as if he is deliberately offering himself up to a catastrophic event. His face—but is it really a face any longer?—is lifted toward the sky.

All this is expressed clearly, without any peculiar characteristics, physically condensed into a general formal unity, raised to a lofty dramatic power and yet controlled by the taut precision of the monumental composition. In spite of the fact that the action is charged with a great intensity, its significance goes far beyond its apparent drama. What, in fact, does this large bronze mean?

Small Miracle. 1951. Bronze. 21 ¼" × 27". Chrysler Art Museum of Provincetown, USA.

Marino's work revolves exclusively around a few themes. One of them is that of the horse and rider, which he incessantly varies and develops. He is well acquainted with the equestrian statues of the past: the ancient Marcus Aurelius of the Capitol in Rome; the gothic Bernabo de Visconti of the Castello Sforzesco in Milan, for which he feels a special esteem; Donatello's statue of Gattamelata in Padua; Verrocchio's Condottiere Colleone in Venice; not to mention the other monuments of later centuries that were raised to the glory of princes and great captains. At the time such statues could be built only for someone who was deserving of them, a sovereign or a victorious hero.

Marino Marini's riders, however, never represent important personalities whose noteworthy deeds are meant to be conserved for posterity. His figures are anonymous. It is precisely in this respect that they are representative of the man who is exposed to the momentous drama of our time.

Marini began with peaceful groups in which man and animal are contrasted. They are conceived as two separate bodies that are related in a complementary way. The horse, which since the beginning of time has been endowed with a special nobility, waits (attentive and confident) for a sign from its master, who tranquilly looks around himself while holding the reins (not shown) in his hands. Marini's most typical work in this style is entitled *The Pilgrim* (1939). In a later work the horse's neck is stiffened and its head is thrust forward, as if it sniffed something unknown. Man raises his head as though he anticipated a supernatural apparition. The theme seems to develop in this way out of itself. Terrified, the horse lifts its head up which the rider holds on to with two hands.

Then he spreads his arms out in an ecstatic gesture, as if he were giving himself up to an unseizable apparition, which he humbly accepts. The emphasis of the horizontal lines relates this crucifix-shaped gesture to the world in a firm, assured way. Marino Marini first gave this work the name of *Resurrection* "as a symbol of the hope and gratitude that overwhelmed me shortly after the war ended." Later he changed the title to *The Angel of the City*, which has the sense of an invocation.

But unknown and unseizable elements draw closer and closer in the terrifying form of their anonymity that surges up from everywhere and nowhere. The head, uplifted, is fixed on the ground as if it wanted to take root and find its salvation there. Terrified, the horse rears and the helpless rider, tossed backwards, loses his balance and seems about to fall. In this way are expressed the insecurity and precariousness of an existence that has gotten out of control. The internal development of the theme reaches its conclusion in 1951. Although physically separate, man and animal are brought together by the composition. The head of the falling horse lies flat on the ground, its hindquarters jut upwards, and its legs risk to give way. Although the rider is thrust backward his feet still rest solidly on the ground. This is the first representation of the *Miracle*, which came to life simultaneously in two versions (one in which the creature falls, the other in which it rears).

In Marini's subsequent work (1953-54) horse and rider are brought even more closely together. The rider, however, lies stretched out lengthwise, impuissant and armless, the unresisting victim of an unfathomable power. Immediately after this "study" (as Marini insists on calling it), a large work was done in bronze (1953-54) and a related one in wood (1954). The rider has now pivoted on himself and his short arms rest on the horse's hindquarters. It is as if he were seeking to avoid or to save himself from an imminent catastrophe.

Small Miracle. 1953. Bronze. Height: 17 ³/₄". Mr. Sanders Coll., Schiedam-Rotterdam.

His bearing is steadier and in it can be read a spirit of affirmation and revolt against the dominant power. This is why the dynamic arch formed by the rear end of the animal strains upwards. The horse looks fearfully at the emptiness in front of it.

In the Munich version in bronze and wood that was executed in 1960-61, Marini returned to the project of 1953-54. Hence the action in both versions is similar, except that it is condensed and modified in the later one. The attitude is no longer one of defense but on the contrary shows a readiness to accept what cannot be understood. The horse has succumbed: death can clearly be seen on its deformed head. The rider is silent. Faceless and armless, without any movement or force, he is nothing but a body thrown backward whose position harmonizes with the animal's. There is no resistance to fate on his part, no question that can be asked. Movement and forms are confronted with nothingness.

A comparison with the 1954 work shows that the more monumental impression is due to the larger scale. The subject brings about a definitive solution, a conclusion.

The first version of the *Miracle*, with respect to the composition and the background, is dominated by a brutal diagonal. In the second, the abrupt vertical of the horse pulled upwards is determinant. The most energetic action is opposed to a passive collapse. Violent verticals are fused in abrupt pyramids. Equilibrium is suddenly replaced with movement. The animal has grown; he rears up like a last cry above all of nature. Closer to the origins than man, he is called by a powerful, immemorial instinct to respond in a way that goes beyond fear and anguish.

Uprooted, his own courage lost, man is exposed to a similar challenge which he is no longer able to meet. In spite of his knowledge and the accumulated strength of generations, he is no longer anything but an abandoned being, a wretched nonentity. The normal scale of size is neglected. The rider becomes small, insignificant. He is defenseless, helpless; it is as if destiny no longer respected him. He begins to topple over but manages to hold on with his thighs; he slips and finally does not fall. Hung vertically, like a rag, on the imposing horse's head, he dangles above emptiness. This second version of the *Miracle*, through its dramatic posture and plastic form, has an extraordinary power and an enduring presence.

Marini began as a painter and draftsman and makes numerous pictures and drawings to prepare his plastic themes. This is surprising if one thinks of the abstract tendency of his works. Nevertheless, it is not a question either of projects or sketches, or of studies done with a specific aim in mind. The themes serve as a starting point around which he plays freely, and they are often enriched

Miracle. 1953. Bronze. 100 $^{7}/_{16}$″ × 31 $^{1}/_{2}$″ × 31 $^{1}/_{2}$″. Museum of Modern Art, N. Y.

Miracle. Study. 1953/54. Bronze. 40 $\frac{1}{8}$″ × 25 $\frac{5}{8}$″. Kunstmuseum, Winterthur.

with many figures as on a stage. It is, in short, genuine painting, with the value of the hypotheses it suggests and of the contours and their relationships. Its only "limitation" is simply that of its involvement with either figurative or abstract representations. Without the slightest reminiscence of or reference to what he has done in painting, the artist then gives life to the sculptural form.

Marini continued to work on and develop the theme of the *Miracle*. He found new representations, new solutions. In 1956, then in 1957-58 and 1964-65, more profound, abstract versions were born. In them horse and rider are now only sketched. Their bodies are fused together in a massive way. The animal and human characteristics subsist in a gloomy expression.

In the fifties Marini called many of his works "Compositions"; in the sixties, to give more clarity and to emphasize the general validity and independent value of the formal representation, this title was changed to "Form in an Idea." From 1968 on, Marini worked almost only in stone. Once again he took up the two versions of the *Miracle*. However, the new material was not solely responsible for transforming the artistic expressions that he has worked constantly on since 1951. Not only is the form now contained in a compact block, but the themes are also condensed. For the second version in stone of *Concept of the Miracle*, Marini used a height of a little more than seven feet whereas the bronze reaches twenty-seven feet. In both works the horse's hindquarters are still conceived only as a pedestal out of which the abrupt form surges. The horse's forelegs have been reduced to stumps. Man has become a separate and

68

Marino Marini at Querceta (Lucca) in the Henraux workshops working on one of his most recent sculptures: "Intuition" 1972, gray stone, 81 ¹/₂″ × 63″ × 39 ³/₈″. (*Photo Amendola*).

Miracle. 1954. Bronze. 46 $\frac{7}{16}$″ × 64 $\frac{9}{16}$″ × 28 $\frac{3}{4}$″. Kunsthistorisches Museum, Vienna.

unarticulated horizontal form, a visual compromise, an "Idea of an Image," a warning sign of time. In 1972 Marini carved two works in stone of the first version of the stricken horse. The first, a *Small Miracle*, is a massive block in which the bodies are inseparably welded together and can only be recognized as vague outlines; the second, an *Idea for a Miracle*, is a large stone whose surface is roughly worked and, here and there, left in a raw state; the signs written on it, the allusions, traces, accents, "spectral fossils" (Marini), have a convincing force.

The riders of Marini have no past which they can refer to. They thus have neither the comfort that comes from lived experience nor the compassion that comes from faith. "My equestrian statues," as Marini himself has declared, "express the torment caused by the events of this century. My state of mind in saying this is close to that of the Romans who, at the end of the Empire, watched a century-old order collapse under the impact of the barbarian invasions. I believe very seriously that we are approaching the end of a world." And in another passage: "The disasters that the riders succumb to resemble those that destroyed Sodom and Pompeii. What I want to do is to portray the last stage in the dissolution of a myth, of the myth of the heroic and victorious individual, of the 'uomo di virtù' of the humanists. My works of these past fifteen years do not wish to be heroic, but tragic. I want to express something tragic, a sort of twilight of humanity, more a defeat than a victory." And to the question: "What could still happen today?" Marini responds: "I don't know. Perhaps we have to go back to the beginning and start out again from there."

This tragic sense is not only related to the theme, by whose transformation and continuous development it is intensified, but it also impregnates every detail of the execution. The more the animal is stricken, the more impuissant man becomes before the fatal force of chance. As well, the plastic vigor, with respect to the restricting space, is affirmed even more resolutely. There is no question here of forms that are taken apart or decomposed, but rather of solid and palpable volumes, of clear rhythms and high stylization. The figures are set in taut contours, and the imprecision of this space

◁ A Form in an Idea. 1964/65. Bronze. Height: 79 $\frac{1}{2}$″. Property of the artist.

Miracle. 1959/60. Bronze. 66 $^9/_{16}$" × 50 $^3/_8$" × 110 $^1/_4$". Kunsthaus, Zurich.

contrasts with the hollows, fissures and cracks that Marino Marini seems to clothe and to fill with suffering like wounds. The same holds true for the surface whose texture and modulations are due to the chance of the casting process. Marini digs into it, tortures it; as he himself says, he activates it until the bronze begins "to breathe." The life of form is in this way opposed to the fall.

Marini gave these works the name of *Miracle*. What does this "miracle" consist of? It is interesting to recall the event thanks to which Saul became Saint-Paul, which is represented in famous pictures by Raphael, Michelangelo, Brueghel the Elder, Rubens and Caravaggio; often, too, it is shown under the aspect of a falling horse. Jesus appeared to the impious one; He spoke clearly: "Why persecutest thou me? It is hard for thee to kick against the pricks." And Saul trembled and was blinded by the apparition "in order to receive the inner light," as is related in the Acts of the Apostles. Marini's *Miracle* has no intention of being a miracle of conversion and salvation that

dispels illusions and arises from the depths to transform man. In Marini's work there is no Promised Land, no attempt at redemption as it shines behind the terrible images of the Apocalypse. Rather, the miracle occurs in an indescribable place that is located in man's inner self, there where fear has its source from which it flows forth—a nameless, unfathomable fear to which every human being is inevitably and hopelessly exposed. "The reason my riders fall from their horses," Marini says, "is because, like all of us, they cannot master their destiny."

And yet, unmistakably, there is salvation! Because the artist grips this invisible fear and dominates it with his vision and, despite all the obstacles, frees it from the unknown by subjecting it to the shaping force of form. In this way he is able to conjure it and to conquer it. Fear, once embodied in form, dissolves: this is the miracle of art. As Marini says, "One can destroy a world, but this destruction already implies the act of reconstruction."

# THE TRAGEDY OF FORM

*by Werner Haftmann*

Marino Marini sculpted *The Cry* in 1962. This image had obsessed him for a long time: in 1960 he sketched it on canvas. In 1962 he did a small sculptural version (8 ¼″ × 11″ × 6″) that is now in Washington. The same year he executed a larger sculpture (29 ½″ × 45 ½″ × 26 ¾″) of the same motif. These preparatory studies finally resulted in the definitive monumental work that now belongs to the Nationalgalerie in Berlin.

The motif consists of two powerful forms: on the right, the forefront of a falling horse; on the left, the body of a thrown rider whose face resembles a crying mask and whose arm is raised like a standard. The forms are so organically structured that these two parts come together and merge in a single symbol that has an overwhelming expressive force. The monumental quality of the work is not a result of its size but of the way the structure is concentrated in the heavy volumes of horse and rider and in the axes of the raised arm

Small Cry. 1962. Bronze. 8 ¼″ × 5 ⅞″ × 11″. Dominion Gallery, Montreal.

The Great Cry. 1962. Bronze. 66 ¹⁵/₁₆″ × 114 ³/₁₆″. ▷
Nationalgalerie, Berlin.

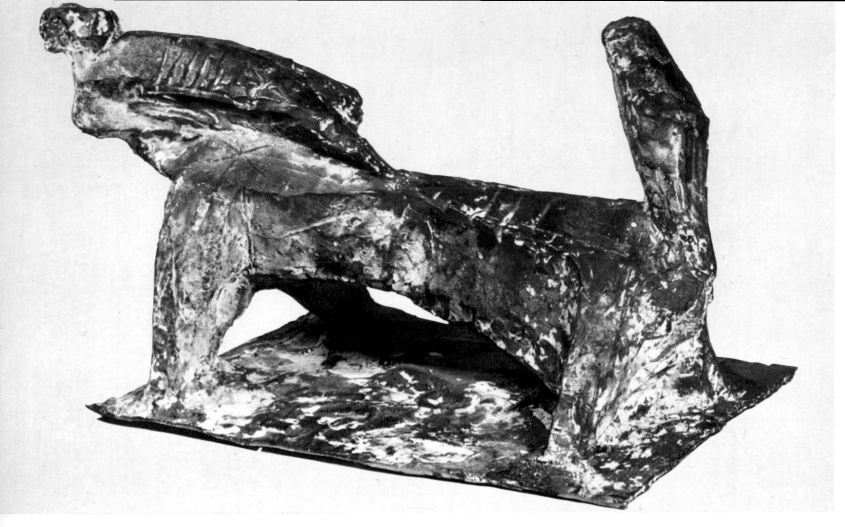

Warrior. 1956/57. Bronze. 8 ¹/₄″ × 14 ⁹/₁₆″ × 9 ¹/₁₆″. Bo Boustedt Coll., Kungälv, Sweden.

Warrior. Study. 1958/59. Bronze. 27 ¹⁶/₁₆″ × 48 ¹³/₁₆″ × 29 ¹/₈″. Galerie Rosengart, Lucerne.

and of the collapsing horse that run through the structural block.

At the dramatic instant that takes place at the height of the fall, horse and rider compose a narrative unity. The juxtaposed surfaces, violently colliding and strangely broken, clearly illustrate the drama contained in the form. The skin of this body made up of horse and rider merged together by destiny has lost its breathing consistency and suppleness and become flayed, wrinkled bark. The fragmented space in which this agony unfolds participates in the drama by means of the outstretched limbs. And the image of the unseated rider becomes the contrapuntal image of a general existential experience through the abridgement of the symbolic signs of expression and through an expressive power that is independent of form and space. Man's condition is reflected in an image of destiny that takes on a strangely mystical resonance.

The image of the rider first appeared in Marini's work in 1936-37. For him it represented the image of man that on account of his Tuscan origins he felt he had inherited from Renaissance humanism. The riders of Donatello or Verrocchio were also familiar to him since his youth. The rider, in fact, became a parable of his experience of life. In 1945, at the end of the war, Marini actually saw them, the riders! They were Italian peasants fleeing the flames of war on their wretched nags, on whose backs they sat in gestures of despair but also of dawning hope. The power of this lived experience transformed the humanist theme into an image of destiny that possessed a great symbolic force—an archaic, mythical image of man fleeing before misery or gloriously asserting himself. Thus, in 1945, the long series of images of riders was born that reaches its apogee with the great rider in the Guggenheim collection in Venice who, his arms outstretched, sits like a powerful cross on his horse.

In 1955 this series was transformed into images of huge falling horses and their tiny thrown riders. In 1960 the series of *Warriors* began and the image of the rider began to fade. He was now rendered only by evocative details and pathetic gestures isolated among the fragments of the collapse. *The Cry* of 1963 belongs to this intellectual context, but this work so full of meaning is the response to an immediate experience of reality.

Marini's riders correspond to the drama that he himself lived. Through them it is possible to see what happened to him and how his perception of life responds to events. This hallucinatory story

The Cry. 1962. Bronze. Height: 29 ½". Mr. Gustave Ring Coll., Washington.

The Theme of the Warrior. 1968. Gray stone. 78 ³/₄" × 39 ³/₈". Mr. and Mrs. Alex Kasser Coll., Montclair, New Y

stands strangely halfway between despair and hope, between acceptance (resignation) and resistance. Marini once said: "My images of riders express the anguish that the events of my time make me feel." He is referring here, of course, to his human preoccupation, and he seeks to depict in his mythic images the menace that hangs over free men today against which he must prepare his resistance. This preoccupation becomes more and more intense in the artist's experience. Its gradual progression is reflected in his work. In the beginning his riders express a vigorous and active image of man; they are young and smiling. But later this strength and éclat diminsh more

and more, and the riders are thrown collapsing horses.

The surface fragmentation becomes the sign reflecting the feeling of man's fragi, the disintegration of form becomes the sy the disintegration of man.

What remains visible is the anguish and l over the disappearance of the great image o sonality that, since the Renaissance, has cr the glory of each century. No one has express this feeling better than Marini himself: "I try to symbolize the final stage in the dissolution of the myth of the great, heroic and victorious personality of the 'uomo di virtù' of the humanists."

# The Pomona at the Uffizi

## by Arturo Bassi

The Buontalenti Room at the Uffizi Museum where Marino Marini's sculpture has just been installed.

On April 29, 1974, one of the three copies of Marino Marini's famed headless Pomona entered the Uffizi Gallery in Florence. This sculpture, which is perhaps the most individual of all the Pomonas, that striking series of female nudes, stands in what is known as the Buontalenti room. It should be underlined that this is the first time that a modern work of art has penetrated into the Uffizi sanctuary which, as everyone knows, is filled with so many masterpieces by Cimabue, Giotto, Piero della Francesca, Leonardo da Vinci, Michelangelo and Raphael. A new masterpiece has thus been added to the sculptures that were brought together by Lorenzo the Magnificent, just as, in its time, Michelangelo's David was integrated into the medieval framework of the Piazza della Signoria.

In his work on Marino Marini, Patrick Waldberg wrote beautifully about these Pomonas, to which no other artist has as yet paid as great a homage. We find it fitting to quote part of his text here:

"I believe that the series of female nudes that Marino has entitled Pomonas correspond to a youthful dream. Later on, Riders, Warriors, Miracles and Cries will display the mark of maturity and show the tragic character of his preoccupations.

Look, then, at these Pomonas of Marino, sometimes swelling at the hips like wine-jars, sometimes lithe and slender, almost ethereal: might one not imagine them standing at the edge of some orchard with goatherds dreaming at their feet under the starry sky of Latium? They give forth the plenitude of the fruit trees they protect, and may be massive, like sleep, or else in a state of alertness, trembling on the verge of the heart's delight. What Marino incarnates in these successive images is woman in her eternal youth ..."

The extraordinary event of the Pomona's entering the Uffizi Gallery was made possible thanks to the efforts of the architect Nello Bemporad, the superintendent of monuments, of professor Luciano Berti, director of the Uffizi Gallery, and of Mr. Luciano Bausi, the mayor of Florence.

I would like to add that I am humbly proud of my own collaboration on this project (from the start of discussions to the final installation), and of the support that the master so generously gave me.

ARTURO BASSI

# Summer in Tuscany

## by Mario De Micheli

Every summer Marino Marini returns to Versilia, to his beautiful house at Forte dei Marmi that, hidden amid the greenery, is far removed from the bustle and excitement of the coast. His friends, his old students from the Brera, the academy in Milan where he taught for a long time, come to visit him here. In Versilia, Marino is truly himself. It is the earth of his childhood, and he used to spend his vacations here in the house of an ex-centric and solitary uncle. It is also his country, Tuscany, to which he is attached by the profound bonds of history and culture. His summers, however, are far from idle.

Every summer he also returns to the large work-yards at Henraux, near Seravezza, where for many years now he has been progressing slowly but steadily in his work on four large sculptures, to be exact, four dark, enormous stones that arrived some time ago from Tunisian shores. A short distance away are the quarries of Michelangelo and the famous white marble statuary that is known throughout the whole world. That is one

Ideal Composition (back view). 1971. Gray stone. 86 ⁵/₈″ × 44 ⁷/₈″ × 39 ³/₈″. Property of the artist. (*Photo Lorenzo Capellini*).

Mr. and Mrs. Alex Kasser Coll., Montclair, New York.
*International Sculpture Exhibition, Rimini, 1971.*
(*Photo Moretti film*).

fact, from 1934-35 (*The Young Woman, Gaby, Paolo*, a *Bacchus*, a *Bather*). But he interrupted the experience rather quickly, not so much on account of intrinsic difficulties as on account of contingent reasons. In truth, stone is an elementary, primitive material, and Marino is fully aware of all its suggestive power and its intimate correspondence with his own poetics. This is why he decided to tackle it again in these four Versilian sculptures.

Unlike modelling plaster, a material that is more docile and also more familiar to Marino, as he used it to execute his greatest works in bronze—and they represent a summit in contemporary sculpture upon which they have had a deep influence—, the relation with stone is one of a direct confrontation. The plastic imagination must play within the limits of something that is already there; it must "invent" inside this thing and impose its own laws. Every true sculptor knows he must harmonize his own creative freedom with the inescapable necessity of the material facing him.

It is thus natural that Marino acted according to this law in his relationship with the stones and that he took into consideration the particular properties of each block—the grain, color, veins, dimensions and other special features. It was in this spirit of unity that he imagined, carved and built up his images, which, although they are in harmony with the stone, inevitably form a contrast with it that violates its geological integrity.

In the large vertical block one of the *Miracles*

kind of marble that Marino feels no affection for: the way it has been used since the nineteenth century for official and funerary monuments, especially in Italy, makes it hateful to him. He readily agrees that other sculptors might enjoy working with it and might be able to create masterpieces out of it but, insofar as he is concerned, he prefers stone. "Stone," he likes to say, "is less noble but more human and more profound because of its anfractuosities and its color."

So, every summer, Marino works the stone. He starts work at eight in the morning (seven hours in the sun). In the landscape of gigantic marble blocks that surround them, the four stones have an unusual presence and stand out like an exception to the rule. Invariably a worker is already there, waiting to assist him. And until it becomes too hot, the dialogue resumes between Marino and the hard images that begin to be outlined and defined in the pieces of African stone, a dialogue in the true sense of the word as there is a constant exchange of questions and answers between the material and the sculptor. A dialogue that is obstinate, harsh and essential.

Carving the stone is a novelty for Marino in more ways than one. The first examples date, in

Miracle. 1970/71. Gray stone. 89 ³/₄″ × 53 ¹⁵/₁₆″ × 35 ⁷/₁₆″.
Vatican Museum. (*Photo Lorenzo Capellini*).

The Concept of the Miracle. 1971. Gray stone. 94 ½" × 57 ¹/₁₆" × 39 ³/₈". Property of the artist. (*Photo Lorenzo Capellini*).

appears: a rearing horse, a compact mass of twisted, rising power, whose rider is about to be thrown; and then, in another massive and elongated block, there is a *Warrior*, a knot of plastic energies freed from the structural tension of the horse-rider couple on the ground. The third block is sharper, and the taut, tight form of a *Horse and Rider* emerges out of it. Finally, in a smaller block, there is an image of woman, a nude *Pomona*.

Except for the "portrait," all of Marino's fundamental themes may be seen at the Henraux workyard, those themes that during forty-five

years of uninterrupted work and research he has never stopped exploring. But what happens to these themes when they are transcribed into a material like stone?

It is obvious that Marino's poetic "system" has not changed in these sculptures, but they possess a specific quality that clearly distinguishes them from those done either in plaster or bronze. It suffices to look at the two almost finished "blocks," the *Pomona* and the *Miracle*, to see this immediately. These images are invested with a sort of fatal gravity in which their ancient earth origin

Pomona. 1972.
Gray stone.
68 $^5/_8$" × 37" × 29 $^1/_2$".
(*Photo Marina Marini*).

can be felt. But that is not all. Stone and rock are themselves "primordial." Marino has not only conserved this value but succeeded in finding an identity common to both "past" and "present." The geological nature of stone is incorporated with all its prerogatives in a metaphor of rare intensity. The material thus becomes its own metaphor in the definition of the plastic image. In this resides the particular quality of these sculptures. The material remains a direct, unchanged, elementary fact, and its meaning is fully understood by Marino who raises it to the level of expression and integrates it into his work as an essential component.

In my opinion, this is the reason why Marino is so interested by these dark, lead-colored stones with their harsh black crevices, to which he returns each summer. On these stones he traces dark, energetic signs; they serve as references for the size, for the exploration of form seeking the image that must come forth. These problems, less familiar than those of plaster and bronze, delight and stimulate Marino. It is hard, slow work, carried out on the very bone structure of nature. To understand the depth of his fascination and the emotion that governs his direct relationship with the stone that he works, one must hear him talk about the Apennine mountains, hear him describe their ravaged profiles, their wrinkles, and how he "reads" their morphology.

When will these four sculptures be finished? Marino does not answer. Next summer, or the summer afterwards, or the summer after that, perhaps. Now he works on one, now on another, following his inspiration or fantasy. Sometimes, too, his interest in *Pomona* or *Miracle*, which are nearly finished, shifts toward other blocks that are less advanced. Marino is in no hurry. Yet when one looks at these images that are still imprisoned in matter and yet already expressed in the vast light of Versilia, there is one thing that strikes one immediately: their dramatic inspiration, common to all Marino's work in recent years. The *Pomona* herself, who always symbolized physical happiness in the sunny, breathing expanse of nature, rises up less violently at Versilia, as if she were weighed down, as if the promise of fertility contained in her full forms were darkened by an obscure premonition.

Marino said to me one day: "We are born and live the poetry of children, and then life goes by under the sign of tragedy and anxiety ... I grew up in a tranquil climate that, from an aesthetic point of view, was perfect. Then, at one stroke, or almost, I entered the tumultuous world of the twentieth century and gradually, at the heart of this tumult, I modified the form and expression of my sculptures. Men have discovered something that seems to go beyond them, something that has escaped from their hands and become a danger to humanity. The artist feels all that, and it grows

Small Miracle. 1972. Gray stone. 29 $1/_8$" × 29 $1/_8$" × 20 $1/_{16}$". Property of the artist. (*Photo Moretti film*).

inside him, and then he becomes tragic, tragic in an absolute sense. That is why the forms of my recent sculpture are broken: they are the architectures of an enormous tragedy."

These words crossed my mind when I was looking at the *Miracle*, which rises up against the sky at the Henraux workyard. What Marino has brought forth out of the stone is truly a concentrated "sign" of tragedy. A *Miracle*, by whom and for whom? Certainly not a miracle of beatifying salvation, but a miracle only in the sense of an incredible event, a supreme and universal moment in the drama of man. Miracle, then, but above all a warning signal sculpted by Marino. A petrified signal, an image that sums up the destiny of man for the historic time we are living in.

*From* XXᵉ *siècle, no. 39, Paris 1972.*

# Marino at the Scala

## by Carlo Pirovano

"Painting, for me, is the result of color, and color takes me further and further away from real form. The emotion that color gives—its juxtaposition with another color and their relationship—stimulates my imagination much more than does the materialization of the human figure if I have to rely on pictorial means alone."

In Marini's conversation one can always find a basic center around which memories and regrets, doubts and satisfactions, are grouped. The artist, however, never takes up a position in a dogmatic way. A closed cocoon around which silk is systematically wrapped in apparent symmetry might stand as a metaphor for his attitude. But the cocoon is not a perfect sphere, any more than was the egg dear to the wise men of antiquity. The only thing that is really firm and established about Marino is the nucleus of his willpower. The rest is but a web spun of fragile myth and pathetic desire.

It is in this direction that one must look for the ideal meeting point between Stravinsky and Marino. What is important is the emotional link that binds them together. If one attempts to prove a cultural accord between them by seeking out linguistic and semantic resemblances one will inevitably be lost in a swamp of hypotheses with no other exit possible but that of approximate and abstract lucubrations which certain art exegetes are fond of developing for their private use or for that of a few rare and fanatic adepts.

The point of this introduction will become clearer

"The Rite of Spring" at the Scala in Milan, season of 1972/73. (*Photo Giacomo Pozzi-Bellini and Luigi Ciminaghi*).

"The Rite of Spring," for which Marino designed the sets and costumes, was performed at the Scala under the direction of Bruno Maderna. The choreography was by John Taras. The premiere took place in Milan on Dec. 9, 1972. This photo shows the first scene. (*Photo Erio Piccagliani - Teatro alla Scala*).

when I say that a German art critic pretends to have explained Marino's inventions down to the last detail (which is to be very badly acquainted with that singing faun who is the artist) and to have established an axiomatic equivalence between Marino and Stravinsky. Certainly, Marino's familiarity with the great composer dates from a long time; everyone knows the superb portrait he made of him with that diaphanous and aggressive head which reminds me of the phantom of one of those ascetics who a long time ago went to mortify their flesh in the desert in the fashion of Leonardo's Saint Jerome. Marino modelled him in New York in 1950 and in 1951 did a second version that is even more purified and reduced to the essential.

But for the Tuscan sculptor Stravinsky was much more than just a personality that had to be captured for eternity by means of the interpretation of a profile, the construction of planes and that ideal geometry present in all of Marino's portraits. Stravinsky, in fact, represented a subtle exchange with a partly remote world, distant in any case; he was the mythical personification of an adventure that Marino engaged himself in as soon as he left his provincial nest, and that may be described as the adventure of the avant-garde, of Paris and of everything that was condensed and given birth to in that city during the first decades of the century. It was also non-conformity, as well as—to call things by their name—ethnic uprooting and mystical anguish joined to a nature with pagan tendencies. The extreme prudence that the Tuscan had shown during his youth in screening the experiences and the contradictions of thirty years of the avant-garde made him less suspicious with respect to a language—that of music—which, at least on the surface, was not directly related to the center of his personal concerns. Perhaps he

87

also realized that through the medium of painting this sap would end up irrigating sculpture as well.

The *Rite of Spring* that was performed at the Scala likewise represents for Marino, after so many years, the moving and direct affirmation of a frail but complex link, as well as an autobiographical revision of an extreme liberty, like all poetic inventions.

The homage paid to Stravinsky and especially to what Stravinsky symbolizes for the artistic culture of this half-century, was already expressed in a more private way in a portfolio of etchings (whose execution dates from 1968 but that were published in 1972) in which the artist's most familiar themes are raised to a rugged lyrical exaltation with great economy of means.

In the sets he designed for the performance at the Scala, Marino introduced in a very natural way many of the themes characteristic of his recent pictorial and graphic work. The loud triangles of the opening curtain, upon which the dancers' costumes are also based, can be found, red, yellow and blue, in many recent lithographs and etchings published in Paris or in Italy. It seems that Marino used these strictly geometrical cutouts to counterbalance the stormy, excessive impetuosity of the pictorial matter that flows and spills over the ideal spaces that the different areas of color would like to reserve for themselves but that they end up fighting for in an uninterrupted series of superpositions and contrasts.

This succession of irrational outbursts and intellectual measure, of temperament and reason, can clearly be seen in the two high points of the *Rite of Spring* such as Marino emphasized them: in the first part the subtle and at the same time

Maquette for the backdrop of the second scene in "The Rite of Spring."

The second scene of "The Rite of Spring" at the Scala. (*Photos Erio Piccagliani - Teatro alla Scala*).

violent thrust of natural forces is translated into volutes and spirals that are recomposed in an affirmed dynamic equilibrium. In the second part, on the contrary, when the theme of "civilization" should emerge (which Marino evokes by the well-known motif of horse and rider), the equilibrium seems to come undone, to fall apart, and the relationships appear less fluid and natural. The warm symphony that the curtains and the backdrop formed in the first part seems to be frozen into a greenish, almost spectral, tonality. A grotesque counterpoint, undoubtedly, but that permits Marino to attain precise dissonances that bear the most profound meaning of the *Rite of Spring*, that blend of stupor and of desanctification that belongs to the spirit of primitive humanity. The sarcastic reminder of the trumpets and flutes of ancient forests is thoroughly familiar to those who have glimpsed, between the foliage, blossomed *Pomonas*. For Marino, the transition from myth to reality and from reality to myth is a natural operation, a spontaneous equivalence.

With respect to the actual performance, it should be noted how much (especially in the first part) Marino's images are based on a new choreography that has very little in common with the classic choreography of the famous Ballets Russes from before the First World War but that shows the trace of an American style unquestionably influenced by the frenzy and rhythm of black dances. This does not happen without some stridencies and a few inelegant moments, but it has the merit of revealing certain underlying elements of Stravinsky's music. The lighting, obviously, was focused on the dancers, with the unfortunate result that the incandescent whirlwinds and bright color areas in Marino's backdrops were not utilized to the maximum of their potential effect.

*From* XX<sup>e</sup> siècle, *no. 40, Paris 1973.*

# Around Brera

## by Alberico Sala

The artist and his wife.

Marino Marini is Milanese in the Stendhalian sense of the word. Milan is a city that, despite a capricious lack of understanding, he slowly wooed and won, just as one might a woman. Marini's first encounter with Milan dates from about 1929 and took place on the Via Monza in that school where the young artist from Pistoia came to replace Arturo Martini. The latter, who came from Venice, had also found in Milan the artistic climate that suited him, the intellectual stimulation and the contrasts that set his creative energies in vibration.

Marino Marini recently completed his conquest of Milan by an extraordinarily generous gesture, the present of a lover to his capricious mistress. It consists of an important collection of his works which presents a complete panorama, from a human as well as a stylistic viewpoint, of his art. This was made possible, it should be said, by the kindness of Marina Marini, the inseparable companion of Marino's life and work, in which she has shared so deeply that she is able to seize and understand the most secret workings of her husband's meditative and creative process. The festivities that took place in honor of Marino Marini's donation also gave me an opportunity to realize the harmony of the couple they form, in the biblical sense of: that the two become one person. Obviously, too, Milan will gain a great deal from having a Marino Marini museum.

How many times we must have taken the road that leads to the Tuscan restaurant on the piazza Mirabello! Marino and his wife always sit at the same table in a room that is a little removed where their friends come to greet them. The happiness of Marino finds a perfect echo in that of Marina, in a sort of spontaneous identification which is, in reality, the fruit of many years of shared trials and certitudes.

Their house stands a short distance away on the edge of the Brera neighborhood, that is to say, that of the Scapigliati, of Manzoni, of Porta. Brera is representative of the best that Milan has to offer. The spirit of Milan is present in the numerous small restaurants that enliven the streets and the squares, and the neighborhood is constantly enriched by the visits of foreigners and by many cultural exchanges. The windows of their apartment open onto the greenery of a small square that bears the name of an admiral who was born in Tortona and was so successful in his naval exploits that he returned a senator!

It is touching to see how much an authentic citizen of the world, which he is as much by his numerous travels as by the presence of his sculptures in all the major capitals, is at home in the town of Brera. Even more than that, he is one of Brera's most distinguished assets, and onlookers take pleasure in recognizing the couple when they are seen walking around their house. Nearby is a rather dry space that nonetheless has a fountain which recalls a curious poem by Palazzeschi and has, indeed, a sick look. On this site a monument was supposed to be built to the memory of someone whose name I have forgotten. Fortunately, this projects was abandoned, either to preserve the withdrawn character of this place, which is more French or even English than Italian—as if such an ordinary intrusion could change it—, or else perhaps because the muncipality wished to reserve this space for a work by one of the greatest modern sculptors. If a sculpture ever stands in the shadows of the trees, it will obviously be one by Marino Marini.

Many people, artists, photographers, journalists, writers, seated on the benches or in cafes, or others strolling in the shops, would all then have an opportunity to see this sculpture and to appreciate in their own way the sensibility and the balance it expresses. What a radically different experience this would be from seeing the upsetting forms of anomalous materials that are abandoned sometimes for months in the grass that borders Milan's streets.

Milan is a city that is either covered by fog or drenched in sunlight. She is fortunate to receive the magnificent portraits that Marino Marini has made of his contemporaries. But, in truth, this generous gesture should have further consequences. It should incite the authorities to bring together in the same place all the donations or acquisitions relevant to those artists who created Italian art. I am referring here to those who have lived or are still living in Milan. But the muncipality, because of its endless decision-making process, falls short of the goals it should set for itself. Milan is, after all, an important center for contemporary art in the world today. Thanks to Marino Marini, this problem has been raised again and given a new urgency. It is time to put an end to all the administrative and political tergiversations. Evidently a building for this purpose has already been purchased by the state, but the necessary work has not yet begun.

We should be grateful not only for the presence of Marino Marini in Milan but also for the meaning of his gesture. All true lovers of art are in his debt, especially those who believe that art, to remain vital, must not be detached from its social context but that, on the contrary, it must contribute to improving the quality of life and to making life more livable.

Marino Marini's workshop in Milan.

91

# A Life in Images

## by Elda Fezzi

"Biografia per immagini," published by Albra Editrice in Turin, is a visual presentation of the life of Marino and Marina Marini. The book consists entirely of photographs taken by the artist's wife. It is thus a diary in images and although the events it records are not free of subjective emotion, it is nonetheless an historical and critical document. It is "critical" to the degree that criticism permits of a certain complicity, an ability to enter into those privileged moments of human experience that influence the work; it is "historical" in the sense that the visualized history gives a concrete measure of the interrelationships between the artist's life and his work and shows in fact the life of a man struggling with matter, his tools, his models, his environment, people, forms, figures, in short, the very object of his research, until finally this object is "brought to light."

The expression does not seem to be irrelevant. Although some of antiquity's criteria as regards sculpture are still valid, sculpture today would be better defined as a dynamic idea that has the power to produce new beings, objects and figures out of stone. Marina's photos make us feel that Marino is engaged in a real dialogue with his "Shadows and Figures." The contact is so strong that it is as if the reader were able to participate vicariously in the metapsychic convulsions of the author as she struggles with her own "emanations." The most extraordinary aspect, both human and full of humor, of everything that Marina puts on view—which is composed like excerpts from films by Alberto Scarabisio—comes from those sequences that seem to wink at the reader, for instance, the subtly phantasmal series of small photos. Here it is possible to see the astonishing quality of an eye that is attentive and sharp and able to discern the intimate life that takes place between the sculptor and his creations. Marina, however, does not feel the temptation to "mythify," but she knows how to seize the "mysterious" aspects of everyday life that man in turn relates to that part of himself, born out of his own depths in such a way that the works he creates are very much those of "homo faber" and "homo ludens," of the builder and the juggler, the sorcerer and the medium. It is as if Marina did not wish to explore the internal values of the different sculptures or to extract their themes, any more

than she wished to deify the sculptor. This is why what she shows us constitutes a sort of familiar lexicon simply because it was lived next to the artist while he was working. The result is a feeling of immediacy. We can follow the artist in the various stages of his creative process, made up of distance and surprise, as he moves between plasters and colors, between the different materials out of which a form is just about to emerge, whether that of the *Pomonas*, the faces of visitors, or that of the *Horses* and *Riders* which are so dynamic and yet have been fixed forever in a miraculous and precarious balance.

"Sometimes," Alberico Sala writes pertinently, "with a great deal of elegance, patience and courage Marina succeeds in involving herself in the creative process by capturing the decisive moments. This does not prevent her curiosity from reaching into the corners of daily life, from showing the artist outside his workshop, on the beach, among the trees of the coast, or with children. Thus, in an age of blatant statements and obsessional images (from audiovisual to posters) Marina has succeeded in making a portrait of Marino Marini both as a man and an artist and in showing how the two, under the effect of multiple influences, are able to counterbalance each other. Among others, the influence of the Etruscans may be mentioned, of whom Marino asked in the ardor of his youth: "Make me live like a young boy, make me live like an artist."

Throughout this "film-book" the reader is completely imbued with the "thoughts" of Marino Marini as well as with the lyrical observations of his sister Egle (Ernesto Caballo has written a masterly introduction). The whole can be described as a "poetical-visual" story that opens with the delicately faded photos of early childhood—Marino and his parents, Marino and his sister—, continues on to his youth and then enters the world of his old and recent work, from the archaic "nudes" to the intense rhythms of his new pieces, all of them charged with "contained force," as Egle Marini puts it.

But let us come back to our first idea, to that metapsychic atmosphere that, thanks to the sensibility of Marina and her gift of observation, surrounds Marino's life and work. In particular, a large, dark, full-page photo stands out at the

A page from the book by Marina Marini ▷
"Biografia per Immagini."
(Turin: Albra Editrice, 1972).

« Questa preparazione pittorica
vien sempre prima del fatto della scultura:
c'è un'idea e ci sono già tante idee.
Dipingendo, le elabori e crei una composizione,
arrivi all'essenza.
Quando hai l'idea sicura, passi a scolpire ».

A page from "Biografia per Immagini."

beginning of the book. The ghostly body and expansive and yet concise graces of the *Pomonas* appear softly against a dark background; it is as if they were held in thrall to a desire for a new life cycle. "The impetuosity of life," the "impetuosity of power" that Marino talks about is specially evident in the keenly rendered truth of the *Portraits* ("the portrait consists less of direct expression than of the slow mixture of the conscious and the unconscious"). Another series of photos shows us works full of Etrusco-Roman reminiscences—a proof of the vitality and lastingness of an old aesthetic. Yet another group of photos translates all the anguishing presence of the "unconscious," particularly in the admirable portraits of Lucosius, 1935, Germaine Richier, 1945, Riccardo Jucker, 1950, Henry Moore, 1962, Jean Arp, 1963, and of so many others, the plaster or terracotta versions of which have just been donated by the artist to the Galleria d'Arte Moderna, Milan.

In the workshops where he habitually works, whether in Milan, Locarno, Forte dei Marmi or else in the foundries, Marino Marini always remains in contact with a "material" that is his own, as he does with the objects and presences that he has made his. It is as if he laid his hands on their hands; he talks to them and rests with them. They are his real companions. It is then that Marina resumes her slow and vigilant investigation, also bringing in one after the other the witnesses of Marino's work, art historians and art lovers (Venturi, Palluchini, Hammacher, Waldberg, Haftmann) as well as contemporary artists (Moore, Arp, Lipchitz, Azuma). The photographic rhythm becomes more taut and dynamic when it is a question, for example, of a conversation with Moore. Marina illustrates this conversation by means of violently contrasted lighting so as to translate its agitated character. On the one hand can be seen the singularly Italian fullness of the Mediterranean who shapes all of his gestures and, on the other, the slow and grave attitude of the English sculptor. It is no more than a simple conversation, and yet its deliberately contrasted character shows in a typical way the relationship between recent Italian sculpture and that of other countries. In the final sequences we discover the meaning of Marino Marini's most recent works in stone. That meaning emerges out of the "great imprecise world of forces," out of the mysterious energy of the Earth-Mother whose forms have been so well rendered by Henry Moore. Truly, it is here, in the center of the same original anguish, that Marino meets Moore.

◁ A photo of Marina and Marino Marini at Tenero in 1943, published in "Biografia per Immagini." (*Photo Bettina Dubini*).

95

# Marino Marini, Painter

## by Patrick Waldberg

By virtue of the considerable room it takes up in his overall achievement, Marino's painting calls for a separate discussion. While it is true, with him, that in the majority of instances painting and sculpture are interrelated, it would also appear that, chronologically, the painting tends almost always to come first. Reviewing the whole of the painted work, one notices everywhere the same cohabitation of ancient soul and modern tremor as in the sculpture, but finds a yet greater freedom of exploration. Very natural causes make for this difference. Sculpture, which is articulated in three-dimensional space, obeys laws of equilibrium which restrict forms to within certain limits. Upon a painted surface, on the other hand, there is

Giselle. 1923. Oil on wood. 24 13/16″ × 19 11/16″. Loaned by Marina Marini to the Galleria Civica d'Arte Moderna, Milan.

nothing to prevent forms from breaking loose and defying any law. The primordial importance Marino accords to painting and his deep attachment to it are attested in his own words.

"For me," he has said, "to conceive of a form is to perceive a vision of color, ardor of life, ardor of form. It's in colors I have looked for the point of departure for each idea which was to become a reality. Painting is to place oneself in the poetry of action; and action in coming about becomes true."

In a general way, all we have observed with regard to Marino's sculpture, its connections with the Etruscan genius, the fusion it embodies of very ancient rhythms with an immediate feeling of the visible world, all these characteristic features of Marino's art recur in his painting, save only that the plastic imagination shows more in the forefront and more sharply here. Once again, this quickening of the dramatic which is perceptible in the painting may perhaps be ascribed to the added freedom this two-dimensional art allows. But I would rather tend to think that Marino has systematically used painting as a means for probing in new sculptural directions.

And so when one considers his most formally audacious sculptures—I have in mind the rider in the act of falling, his body leaning dangerously to the left while his right leg kicks in midair; or else the thread-like horse, held erect by its structural scheme alone—these are regularly preceded by one or several paintings in which it seems the artist has tried to evaluate the eventual risks of a sculptural transcription.

It is important to remember that Marino's first years at the Academy were devoted exclusively to painting and drawing. Hence, it is the fruit of considerable experience and of an already well advanced maturing that he puts before the public when he gives his first show of paintings. Those of the years 1929-30, of a sensitive and vibrant classicism, radiate a natural charm that one is tempted to call unconscious, so much does it seem that their serene, self-assured beauty has been obtained without effort or hesitation.

The dramatizing of forms appears, however, in the couples and the trios—in for example the *Pomona* couples, after 1940—or in certain haunted, violent, impassioned compositions, such as the *Dream and Reality* of 1950. In connection with the later periods in Marino's work some have spoken

Orpheus. 1956. Oil on canvas. 96 $\frac{1}{2}$″ × 118 $\frac{1}{8}$″. Property of the artist.

Blue Rider. 1955.
Oil on canvas.
55 $\frac{1}{8}$" × 33 $\frac{7}{8}$".
Emilio Jesi Coll.,
Milan.

Black Miracle. 1954. Mixed media. Paper mounted on canvas. 50 $^3/_8$″ × 33 $^7/_8$″. Private coll., Milan.

The Carriage Builder's Daughters. 1957. Oil on canvas. 59 $^1/_{16}$″. Loaned by Marina Marini to the Galleria Civica d'Arte Moderna, Milan.

Dancer. 1959. Oil on canvas. 59 $^1/_{16}$″ × 47 $^1/_4$″. ▷
Property of the artist.

Representation in Green. 1958. Oil on canvas. 47 ¼″ × 39 ⅜″. Emilio Jesi Coll., Milan.

Stage Set. 1960. Oil on canvas. 77 $^{15}/_{16}$″ × 66 $^{1}/_{4}$″. Loaned by Marina Marini to the Galleria Civica d'Arte Moderna, Milan.

Passion for the Game. 1967. Oil on wood. 78 ¾″ × 78 ¾″. Property of the artist.

of discordance and even of the decomposition of forms, pointing to the progressive shift from realistic figuration to a more abstract conception. For my part, I do not find any disparity between this or that moment in his work, which, to my eye, display a remarkable homogeneity. And rather than abstraction, it is a stylizing of forms I notice, this stylization serving as vehicle to a new animation through which, into this hitherto calmly meditative work, Marino introduces inner restlessness and anxiety. It is to be noted, moreover, that this troubled mood is expressed in paintings well before it makes its way into the sculpture: the stricken riders were first tried out on canvas and in oils.

Like all the major sculptors, Marino is a draftsman—a draftsman even before being a painter—but what is remarkable in his case is the autonomy of the drawing and painting vis-à-vis the sculpture. Rodin, for instance, expresses himself in volumes when he draws, and it is fair to say that almost all his drawings are studies for sculptures. Marino's spontaneity, the instinctual character of his art have enabled him, to the contrary, to invest each of his means of expression with its own independent style. Thus, the drawn portraits, managed with admirable lightness of touch, stand absolutely on their own and absolutely apart from the sculptured heads they pair with. Striking in these portraits of friends, of fellow-artists, of art-collectors, are the inward dimension of the likeness and, simultaneously, the keenness of the line, sure as the flight of a bird in the sky. They have that rare quality of seeming to owe nothing to technique, to skill, and this to the point where they can only be compared to poets' drawings, for example Baudelaire's of himself or else Verlaine's of Rimbaud in the streets of London.

The gift for apprehending the real is not by any means the commonest thing in today's art. It is certainly at the behest of something profound in him—at the behest, I am prepared to say, of faith—that Marino has cleaved to the figurative forms of representation. It would be absurd and highly unjust to put this down to fighting a rearguard action, or from it to infer a refusal on his part to understand or to accept other modes of expression in art. To the contrary, Marino possesses an open-mindedness which has become rare, and it is evidenced in a statement such as this: "I make no distinction," he declares, "between abstract and figurative plastics, provided that in both cases these be authentically plastic. What counts is the quality of the work. As for me, a Mediterranean man, I cannot express myself freely otherwise than through figures. But I acknowledge and admire all other manners of self-expression." There is much modesty and nobleness in these words and they reveal at the same time Marino's acute awareness of his own situation and of the nature of his art in relation to current trends.

*From* Complete Works of Marino Marini. *(New York: Tudor Publishing Company, 1970).*

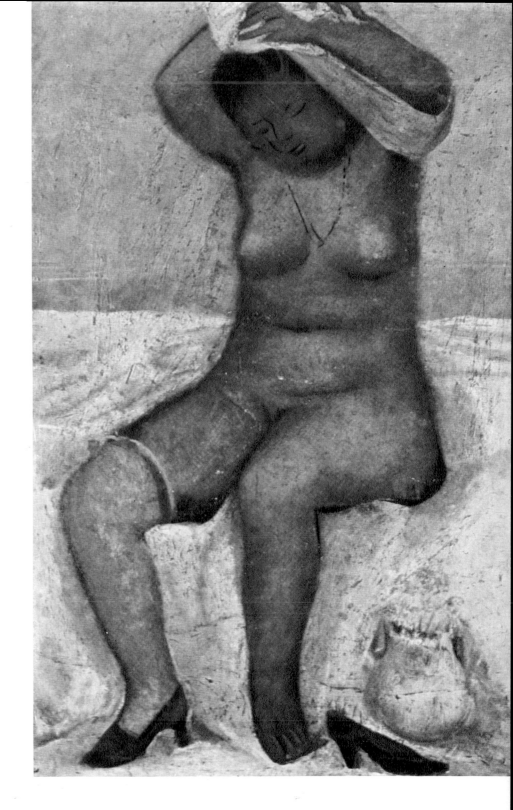

The Algerian Woman. 1927. Oil on wood. 49 $\frac{1}{4}$" × 29 $\frac{5}{8}$". Loaned by Marina Marini to the Galleria Civica d'Arte Moderna, Milan.

# The Graphic Work of Marino Marini

## by G. di San Lazzaro

### The Engravings

Marino Marini was attracted by engraving from his adolescence onwards. Although his early designs as a student are unknown, his etchings from the same period have been preserved. The artists under whose influence he first came were his teachers at the Academy of Fine Arts in Florence and some artists with a purely local reputation—for the city strangely ignored the great European artists of the day. His early works, wavering between Symbolism and Realism, the ephemeral sovereigns of the period, were already marked by the sureness of their composition and the vigor of their line. At that time, Italy remained artistically dependent on Central Europe, in spite of the resounding manifestations of emerging Futurism. Inspiration did not come from Paris but from Munich, and not from the Munich of Kandinsky and Klee but from that of the teachers from whom

these two great innovators had obtained their training. The engravings, as much as his modeling, pictorial or lithographic works, interpret Marino Marini's efforts to free himself from these obsolete influences and to reveal himself to himself. For many years the engravings were not published, for the artist, who created them for his own pleasure, has always obdurately refused to sell them. It was only with the publication of *Idea e Spazio* (1963) and particularly with *Album N. 1* (1968), that it became possible to appreciate to what extent his line could remain individual on a zinc plate and how much more incisive it is in his engravings than in his lithographs, in which he is limited in some degree by the material.

His engravings, therefore, contemporary with his works in other media and based on his favorite themes, are exceptional in the sense that they were carried out in his own workshop (unlike the lithographs on which he had to work with various

Two etchings from the portfolio "Idea e Spazio." Published by the Cent Bibliophiles de France et d'Amérique, Paris, 1963. On the left: Jugglers. On the right: Morning.

Two etchings from "Album N. 1." (Paris: Ed. XXᵉ siècle, 1968). On the left: Invocation. On the right: The Theater of Masks.

Two etchings from the Crommelynck Album, Paris, 1970. On the left: Pomona. On the right: Juggler.

Miracle. Etching from the portfolio "Tout près de Marino." (Paris: Ed. XXᵉ siècle, 1971).

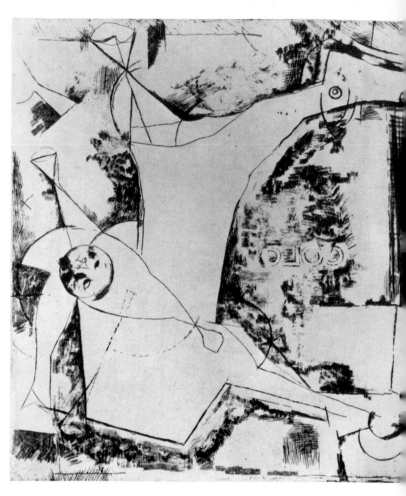

Miracle. Etching from the portfolio "Imagines." (Berlin: Propyläen Verlag, 1970).

Pomonas. Etching from the portfolio
"Tout près de Marino."
(Paris: Ed. XXᵉ siècle, 1971).

printers either in Paris or in Switzerland). The experimental proofs were made either on the small presses of the Academy of Monza or on those of the Brera Academy of Milan (where he was one of their well-known teachers until his resignation in 1968) under the supervision of the laboratory assistant of the Academy. It was necessary to wait until 1963 for the publication of *Idea e Spazio* in which he illustrated the poems of his sister Egle, and then in 1968 for the *Album N. 1*, in order that these zinc plates had the good fortune to be entrusted respectively to the Crommelynck brothers and to Jacques Frélaut (Imprimerie Lacourière).

Since then, we should note the 23 etchings from the portfolio of the Crommelynck brothers (1970), the 10 etchings from *Imagines* (Propyläen Verlag, Berlin 1970), the first etchings in color illustrating the book of Egle Marini *Tout près de Marino* (Ed. XXᵉ siècle, Paris 1971), the 20 etchings and drypoints from *Marino Marini, Opera Grafica* (Luigi De Tullio Ed., Milan 1972), and finally the 10 engravings from *Marino to Stravinsky* (Alba Editrice, Turin 1972). Also, some very beautiful engravings have been published separately for various publishers.

At the end of the introduction to *Album N. 1* I wrote: "It might be worth remarking that Marini's expressive line does not dissolve as it softens in that decorative, abstract or figurative expressionism which is a trap that too many artists, including some of the greatest, have fallen into. Marino's sensuality has not grown thicker or heavier, has not become sexualized, one might say. Its acute vigor can be related to Picasso's In fact, it has been transfigured, grown lighter, acquired an airy transcendence. In the engravings that date from 1950-52, the games of love are no longer anything but a play of shadow and light."

## The Lithographs

For a book written by his friend, the painter-poet Filippo De Pisis in 1941, about his sculpture (Ed. della Conchiglia, Milan), Marino Marini executed his first two lithographs. The following year, having taken refuge in Switzerland and using the lithographic stones of the printer Salvioni, in Bellinzona, he drew nudes, Pomonas, horses and horsemen, bathing them in a delicate chiaroscuro which, far from enfeebling them, affirmed the vigor and purity of forms. It was, however, only after 1951, that his artistry acquired the personal character which places him in the front ranks among the great masters of contemporary lithography. For the first issue of the new series of *XXe siècle*, he engraved his work on ink-coated stone and in this same composition used a little color, very little. However, he immediately abandoned this process and used it only occasionally later to draw freely on stone, either on a plain gray or white background. His art dealer, Curt Valentin, then commissioned him to do a series of seven lithographs, printed by F. Mourlot in Paris. With the exception of a "juggler," he repeated the theme of horses and horsemen, already treated in 1942, but this time his vigorous lines came to life in an irresistible dynamism. We can also find in this series his need for expressive synthesis, at first purely geometric, to which he was to return later and which was, especially in 1952, a reflection of earlier research in the field of abstract painting (1937).

Thus, the mastery of Marino Marini, lithographer, asserted itself in Paris in 1952. The following year he worked in Switzerland with the printer Kratz (today Matthieu), commissioned by Klipstein & Kornfeld for the "Guilde de la Gravure" (directed at that time by Nesto Jacometti), as well as for Gérald Cramer. In 1954, he returned to Paris again, where he executed, with Mourlot, a lithograph in black, yellow and blue for the Art Institute of Chicago, but he returned frequently to Switzerland where he engraved, among others, with the printer Wolfensberger, for the Gallery of Modern Art of Basel, the portrait of Thomas Mann after an original drawing commissioned by the editor, Fischer, for an edition of the complete works of the author of *The Magic Mountain*.

The following year the Berggruen Gallery of Paris paid homage to the works of Marino Marini

The Concept of Virginity.

Rupture.

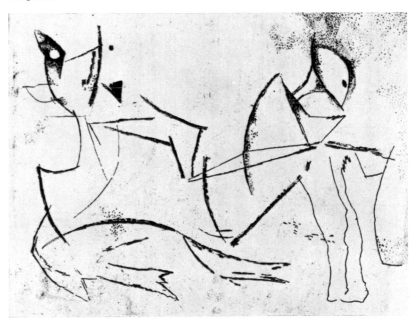

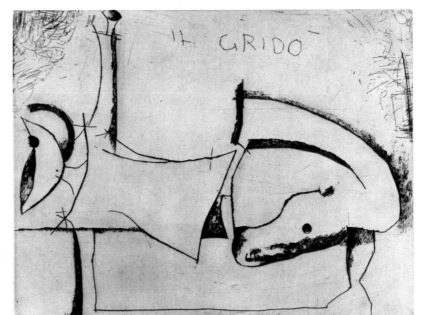

by exhibiting fifteen plates printed in Paris and Zurich, and edited a brochure on the author. The artist drew two lithographs with the printer Mourlot, one for Berggruen, the other destined for the printer himself and which was not sold until 1968. Still with Mourlot, he composed lithographs for Cramer; but did not forget Switzerland, which shares with France the honor of having printed the greatest works of the master's golden age.

In 1957 and 1958, he created four plates for Nesto Jacometti's "L'Œuvre Gravée"; then, after an interruption of two years, he returned to the Kratz Printing House—now under the direction of Matthieu—and worked there for Jacometti and Kornfeld. In 1962, he agreed, for the "Association des Cent Bibliophiles," directed by Madame Madeleine de Harting, to create a few lithographs to illustrate a volume of poems by his sister, Egle. However, he completed only one, with Mourlot, suddenly preferring engraving to lithography. There was a new interruption of three years devoted exclusively to sculpture and painting in which he was becoming increasingly absorbed. In 1965, the theme of the "Miracle" inspired a first lithograph which he gave to the Philadelphia Museum of Art on the occasion of a large exhibition of his graphic works, and he then composed a new lithograph on the theme of the "Miracle" for L'Œuvre Gravée. Most of this work consisted of compositions in black and white that were, in a way, imposed on him by his preoccupation at that time with plastics. However, though black expressed the dramatic power of the theme perfectly, color was not to be forgotten for long. After several lithographs for the Toninelli Gallery, as well as a new plate for *XXᵉ siècle* he undertook the album *From Color To Form* for which he dictated the preface and which includes ten large lithographs printed by Mourlot (commissioned by *XXᵉ siècle* and Leon Amiel, who had already edited jointly the *Album N.1* of engravings printed on the Lacourière presses by Frélaut). Finally, we should note the most recent portfolios published by the Editions *XXᵉ siècle*: *Chevaux et Cavaliers* (1972), and *Personnages du Sacre du Printemps* (1974).

In the words of M. Carandente, author of the introduction to the catalogue of lithographs by Marino Marini (Toninelli Pub., Milan), we can say that "rarely themes as limited in synthetic figurations have found in art vaster possibilities for precise expression." From the first works to the last, from the "Horsemen" and "Pomonas" to the "Warrior" and the "Cry," to the abstract interpretation of "Group of Elements," these themes express "a real adventure for modern visual consciousness." Their force moves from one work to the next by a dramatic, tragic and irresistible impulse and, beyond the novelty of figurative invention, we recapture the notion of something which existed in an absolutely free and eternal visual universe."

Three lithographs from the portfolio
"From Color to Form."
(Paris: Ed. XXᵉ siècle, 1969).

# ENGRAVINGS

... *Marino Marini's use of different techniques, whether that of the fine incision of drypoint or that of the now thick, now mordant line of the etching, is never a mere exercise in virtuosity. A constant control of the expression that is sought after excludes the temptations of "effect." The inevitable result is a vigorous work of the most gripping simplicity. Like his sculptures, Marini's engravings are not satisfied with rendering the capricious appearances of reality; what they aim at, and succeed in doing, is to translate its poetic substance, its message. "The ability to depict reality is certainly not the most widespread quality in contemporary art," wrote Patrick Waldberg. With what mastery, however, whether the line is faint or accentuated, whether it is a question of the radiant luminosity of a white surface or else of the "toccato" of the scratchings and networks, whether it is the multiple intensity of the "shading" or of the "bites," with what mastery does Marino Marini use all the possibilities of an invention taken directly from life.*

... *The engravings provide Marini with a different context in which he transcribes and develops earlier plastic ideas and tests their value and their constant human relevance ...*

... *In the same way, each of these engravings permits us to see the effect the artist was able to draw out of the different expressive possibilities inherent in each technique. Emphatically engraved lines alternate with a fragmented, repeated outline, and this results in "cold" areas of chiaroscuro, in thick, heavy shadows. The figures are drawn against a velvety, almost downy, graphic background. Sometimes, on the contrary, they seem as if crystallized in a metallic light born out of a network of lines ...*

... *What we have just said could be illustrated by many examples, and it would obviously be interesting to compare Marini's graphic work with his sculptures or paintings. It would also be interesting to show the great originality with which he has interpreted graphic science, from Mediterranean classicism to the revolutionary innovations of Picasso.*

*Marino Marini said to me one day, "There is a part of myself that lives in graphic art." His engravings, in effect, permit us to see all the intensity involved in his creative process; in addition, they bear witness to the fundamentally human aspect that is embodied in them ...*

FRANCO RUSSOLI

From *Marino Marini, Graphic Work,* a portfolio of twenty original prints (Milan: Luigi De Tullio Publisher, 1972).

Three lithographs from the portfolio "Chevaux et Cavaliers." (Paris: Ed. XXᵉ siècle, 1969).

Lithograph for the book "Complete Works of Marino Marini." (New York, Tudor Publishing Co., 1970).

Lithograph for the poster of the Olympic Games in Munich. 1972.

# LITHOGRAPHS

...When Marini wishes to express his personal universe by means of lithography, he does nothing but return to his old fondness for a technique which he masters perfectly and from which he is able to draw vivid and beautiful effects. This also permits him to advance more clearly in the expression of certain ideas which usually do not stand out as much in his sketches for a sculpture. It is obvious that Marini's lithographs are not comparable in importance to his sculptures. It would not please Marini, besides, if they were considered as such. But, on the other hand, it would be unjust to see them only as occasional works. His lithographs, in fact, bear witness to a much deeper artistic motivation; they exist in themselves, as works of art that are as independent as they are complete.

There are many modern painters—Degas, Renoir, Gauguin, Matisse, Picasso, Modigliani, for example—who judged it necessary, in order to use all their creative faculties to a maximum, to convert their figurative two-dimensional representations into volumes. In doing this they made an important and unexpected contribution to the world of sculpture. In the case of Marini, on the contrary, we are dealing with a sculptor—comparable in this respect to Maillol, Laurens, Giacometti—who, to escape from the conditioning imposed upon him by the needs of three-dimensional forms, practices those two-dimensional realizations that are characteristic of painting. He thus gives proof of his skill in translating the reality of his vision while at the same time executing an authentic pictorial composition. This is why I would like to underline what, to my mind, is the most specific quality of Marini's lithographs: the audacity of the color, the vibrant sensibility expressed by the lines, all this combined with a very vigorous technique. It is certainly not a question of pretending that Marini's lithographs should be ranked among the major works of modern art, although the graphic conception of these works is indeed revolutionary, whatever the sudden impact of their meaning. But, as for myself, I cannot keep from being fascinated by the dazzling brio of Marini. His lithographs depict at one and the same time both joy and pathos, spirituality and sensuality, to all of which is sometimes added a real sense of humor or, on the contrary, a sudden premonition of latent disaster.

This is the tightrope on which Marino Marini continues to develop with a singularly Italian elegance ...

DOUGLAS COOPER

From *Marino Marini* (Milan: Silvana Editoriale d'Arte, 1959).

Study for one of the eight lithographs from the portfolio "Personnages du Sacre du Printemps." (Paris: Ed. XX<sup>e</sup> siècle, 1974. *Photo Jacqueline Hyde*).

# Tributes

## Paul Fierens:
# MARINO AS A ROMAN

... The Italy of the *Novecento*—whose awakening strikes us as one of the most remarkable and important facts of contemporary art history—has an excellent group of sculptors. In the most original way Marino Marini plays the role of centurion, of *chef de file*. Although he remains in accord with the "tendency" that probably will be considered as being expressive of an epoch and of the spirit of a generation, he also seems to be more and more in accord with his own personality.

.  .  .  .  .  .  .  .  .  .  .  .

Trained in Florence, Marini, for the time being, has become a Roman. He puts the emphasis on the individuality of his models, but he raises that individuality to the power of a "type." He expands the volumes, adds weight to hands and legs, generalizes the expressions, avoids symbols and creates a plastic equivalent of reality that has nothing photographic about it. He yields to the attraction of terracotta by means of which Italian sculpture, having made a vow of poverty, redeems the virtuosities and material excesses that were such a heavy heritage from the past. He twists the neck of eloquence and attempts to speak with calmness and clarity in prose ...

*From* Marino Marini, Art Italien Moderne *(Paris: Editions des Chroniques du Jour, 1936).*

Marino Marini at the age of three. Pistoia, 1904.

## Eduard Trier:
# MARINI AND BOCCIONI

... If we are interested in the relationship between Marini's theories and those of the sculptors that preceded him at a relatively recent epoch, it is important that we take into account the Futurist norms as they were set forth by Boccioni. In paragraph eight of his Manifesto Boccioni declares: "There is no renewal possible outside of a sculpture that is related to the space around it. Only such a sculpture is capable of creating a new plastic form that can develop and expand in space, as if modelling it." (Technical Manifesto of Futurist Sculpture, Milan, April 11, 1912).
Boccioni zealously applied himself to furnishing a scientific demonstration of his theories. The examples he created were meant to be both didactic and intuitive, such as *Development of a Bottle in Space*. Even if his purism and his impetuous soi-disant objectivity made him impermeable to the nature of Marini, which has always been an enemy of such complexities, the artistic formula of spatial expansion—an expansion that consists in decomposing the different planes of a "solid" so as to reconstruct them later around the volume that determined them—this formula is precisely evident in the works of Marini. For example: in the "expanded" limbs of the *Riders*. There is thus a community of expression between the two artists. But, in fact, there is not much in common between Marini and Boccioni's theory, at least on two vital points. First of all, Marini did not let himself be swayed by the Futurists' attempt to give their sculpture a kinetic look. Secondly, he did not accept their other theory condemning a priori all "figures." It is for this reason, and also undoubtedly because of his devotion to the Etruscan past of Tuscany, that he was not influenced by the Futurist cult of the machine. Marini's central theme, the Horse and Rider, asserts a categorical refusal to exalt, as the Futurists did, a civilization obsessed by the machine. The *Horse* and *Rider* of Raymond Duchamp-Villon—two sculptures that were made after Cubist and Futurist dogma—show the deliberate choice of a Constructivism with kinetic tendencies, to which Marini opposes his own faith in architectonic form.

.  .  .  .  .  .  .  .  .  .  .  .

However, neither historical nor biografical investigations are sufficient to "explain" Marini. Rather than relying on an exterior examination of his work, it would be more fruitful to pay attention to the artist's intentions: in other words, we should look for what, in the theme of the Rider, interested Marini as a sculptor.
I believe that the answer is precisely the tension that exists between the static and dynamic forms, so apparent in the *Rider*, and which stimulates Marini's desire to resolve the plastic problem. The two possible solutions—architecture and movement—have both been explored by Marini, who has put the emphasis now on one, now on the other, similar to the way variations are played on the same theme in music. But, most frequently, Marini has attempted to establish an equilibrium between these forces, and it is this that produces the particular tension ...

*From* Marino Marini *(Milan: Ed. Garzanti, 1961).*

◁ Portrait of Mrs. Etienne Grandjean. 1945.
Polychrome plaster. Height: 13 ³/₄".
Grandjean Coll., Zurich.

Marini with his regiment (1924).

# Filippo De Pisis:
# THE LOVE OF FORM

... If I were a philosopher of the serious type and not someone who daubs canvases with paint, I would uphold and exploit the following theory: that the artist and his work are one, that together they constitute a single entity. By this I mean when the artist is a man in the deepest and most immanent sense of the word. In a larger sense, if one considers matter to be undifferentiated—which is virtually proven—one might maintain that the work of art is only one of its emanations. The same holds true for the artist. Here is a brilliant illustration of this theory: the sculptor Marino Marini, a warm person who has already reached a certain maturity and yet seems as young to me as when he first showed up a long time ago in my studio on the rue Servandoni in Paris. It pleases me to imagine that the secret of the incontestable harmony that exists between his talent, his voice, his gesture, his physical person, is due to the land where he was born and grew up, the gentle countryside of Pistoia. The same can be said for the joy he finds in life and his light melancholy which is such an enemy of romantic accents and literary artifices.

. . . . . . . . . . . . .

But let us talk a little about his "portraits," for example, which are so full of life and have such a direct relationship with reality.

I would first mention, among so many other works, one of the "portraits" that truly delighted me: the *Sleeping Bacchus* (1934). This work undoubtedly tempts one to evoke the great classical Greek and Tuscan artists: the theme bears certain resemblances and there is also a certain stylistic similarity. Happily, an unmistakable originality asserts itself. For the character lives and thrives on a completely inner life. With his eyes closed and his elegant body delicately resting, partly covered by a light veil, every detail works to create a perfectly materialized image of sleep and purity. It is almost as if we were able to distinguish the breathing of the sleeping (masculine) beauty.

Donatello, in such a case, would undoubtedly have devoted more attention to the modelling and put more emphasis on the proportions. Rodin would probably have added an excessively "literary" touch and the soft face would have remained stony. It would be easy to write more about this portrait, but there are certain achievements that impose silence.

Much has been said about Marini's youthful works and their relationship with Etruscan art. But their intentional stylistic treatment in no way limits their inspiration or diminishes the life that beats inside them.

There are a few portraits of men that have, it will be said, something caricatural about them, but the artist has nonetheless given them a spiritual resonance, a sort of harshness that remains likeable because it is the characteristic of certain cultivated and tormented spirits. On the other hand, there are many female nudes that are imbued with an ardent but contained sensuality suggestive of creatures glimpsed in dreams. Others, like Ersilia, are clothed and tranquilly seated with their hands crossed on their knees; their full breasts have an admirable sculptural presence. They may be thought of as a successful attempt to poeticize certain aspects of middle-class life ...

The *Traveller* (1939) from the della Lanterna collection shows us, in fact, a twin harmonious figure: that of an equestrian couple, a theme that has always preoccupied artists. An entirely Hellenic grace animates the horse that is both nervous and very moving, as well as the young rider who seems to be an incarnation of purity. This sensation is accentuated in the *Gentleman on a Horse* (1940) in which the style itself is affirmed more clearly.

To return to the "nudes," Marini has never stopped creating beautiful women, women that he himself has called "solar." They almost make one think of the "strong women" of d'Annunzio, but, thank God, Marini's women have nothing literary or artificial about them. In my opinion, the two most beautiful ones are those which belong to the Feroldi collection in Brescia (1940) and to the Pallina collection in Milan (1938). As for Marini's drawings, they can only be described as excellent. Their color is superb; color, it might be added, is a real passion for Marini. A few drawings have a relatively simple graphism; others are more synthetic and alive; still others are covered with close-set, nervous lines. The spirit, however, is always the same.

The love of form has never hurt the cause of poetry. For me, Marini's riders stepped down one bright morning from the Parthenon in order to make themselves more human and to come and ride on the roads of man. If they are still a trifle stiff it is because Marini did not wish to do something that would either be easy or banal. Besides, they soon grow active and it is as if, already, we can hear their horses whinnying from afar ...

*From* Marino Marini *(Milan: Ed. della Conchiglia, 1941).*

Marini, Morandi and Ragghianti, ▷
Venice Biennale, 1948.

## Gianfranco Contini:
# FIRST STAY IN SWITZERLAND

... The feeling that inspires Marini is thus certainly not a general human feeling (the ordinary feeling of a poet), but a very specialized feeling that can only be developed by the practice of art. The pure man of letters might feel understandably uncomfortable in a milieu in which all the locks can only be opened by keys related to specific competencies. But this is not at all the same as saying that Marini can do without myths. The present exhibition is finally but the catalogue of the main myths with which Marini has populated his stay in the Tessin since 1942. The sparkling air of the pre-alpine lakes, the mountains which are both steep and friendly, the tranquil vegetation—the whole landscape that Marini dominates from his Tenero workshop—would be felt by any man from the North as a foretaste of the South, the first notes of the trumpet sounding the Mediterranean fanfare ...

*From* 20 sculpture di Marino Marini, *with a preface by Gianfranco Contini. (Lugano: Ed. della Collana, 1944).*

The artist and his wife with Curt Valentin (1954).

## Raffaele Carrieri:
# SPACE AND FORM

... Marini's drawing invariably contains the origin and principle of the form that will come forth. Form is here in its first stage, a formless form, both ethereal and animal. It exists as a necessity and a probability, an indefinite number. It is a seed, a germination, an erection. Space suddenly contracts to receive the discharge of the first contact, of the first line. Space is condition and dimension. In it everything is possible: silhouettes, reflections, reality. The meteor stamps it with its imprint, like a vertiginous corolla. The sphere fills it with its shadow. The clear, airy flight of the dove unhesitatingly traverses it, guided by its madness. The sketch is cut up and becomes image. An abstract divinity materializes itself. A divinity or an element from the vegetable world, a plant, the moon, a head of hair, a horse, man and woman. A throng of things, as similar as they are dissimilar in the geometrical order: lines and circles appear like so many organic forms, women as well as horses. Here are women and horses progressing hesitantly, linked together in a network of very fine lines, taut or loose, but all living and expanding like nerves across an eyeball. In the rapid voyage of the line, there is not a form that is not itself. The line, in its aerial flight, captures all the positive values. It turns them into outlines and volumes. The game then continues in broad daylight. It resembles a meticulously choreographed ballet of phantoms: jugglers, acrobats, horses. Horses and riders, seen in profile, in every stage of development, in every possible combination. Some are immobile, caught in a fabric of edges and éclats which have an oppressive relief. Or else they stand in perspective like simple structures, like horse-sharks, horse-spheres, as light, however, as young boys dashing out of the surf. Marini's horses and riders, with their lunar faces and their impenetrable look ...

Marini's drawing is not only linear and curvilinear, nor is its task confined to profiling silhouettes. Freed of rules and of obedience to any school, it can, if it likes, cluster together or disperse itself depending on the caprice of the masses, of their agglomerations and reliefs. It is a drawing whose genre is not limited. It is born instantly out of the necessity to communicate; it can be broken or continuous, sinuous, complex or massive. The figures are enveloped by a dense network of signs. Inside this network bodies move freely, are modelled, absorbing the exact quantity of light and shadow that is necessary to bring forth the plastic rhythm. The nudes are superimposed and become compact. The scene resembles that of after a massacre. To attain a static state, one hundred figures are activated. The great hieratic quality of the *Pomona* comes from all this movement, all these spaces, these evolutions, all this "doing" and "undoing," all of which takes place ceaselessly until the final goal is achieved: that single and incorruptible body ...

*From* Marino Marini *(Milan: Ed. del Milione, 1948).*

(*Photo Marina
Marini, 1963*).

Lamberto Vitali:
# A THREATENED CIVILIZATION

... The destiny of Marino Marini resembles, in numerous aspects, that of many other artists. This is particularly true in our turbulent and uneasy times. Don't artists have a gift to foresee social turmoil, political crises, the disasters of war? It can even be said that in this respect they have an insatiable, almost demoniacal, curiosity. They want to explore everthing, to know everything, from primitive popular arts to those of the East. They show a clear preference for ancient civilizations. They have a need to absorb and to transform everything that they see and sometimes even to deform it. Such a ravenous appetite, it must be admitted, is characteristic of a civilization that has reached its full maturity, perhaps even its final phase. What sometimes seems like the advent of a new art is only—and I believe that in saying this I am not yielding to a pessimistic bias—the last manifestation at the end of a period, a manifestation that resembles a very rare, extremely refined flower but is in reality the product of a new Alexandrinism. Thus, an artist among artists, a man among men, Marino Marini lives and must live in the atmosphere of his time. It is even completely natural that he does not escape

from the general tendency and lets himself be borne along by an irresistible current.

It is enough to look at his work to see the sources that the artist draws his inspiration from, now in a deliberate, now in a probably unconscious way. The plastic arts of ancient China, of Egypt, of Greece and Rome, seem to represent for him a sort of anthology. If one so desired, it would even be possible to single out each of the sources of his inspiration. But what would be the point of such an inquiry? What is important is to establish that the ideas that inspired him have not just been restituted in an inert form but, on the contrary, have been infused with new life. What is important is to see the effects of Marini's creative power, which is strong enough for him to permit himself such dangerous relationships. In other words, what should be recognized is his ability to transcend the "charm" of his models and attain his own individual form of expression. But what is Marini's intention? I have said in the past and will say again now: the art of Marini consists in the architectonic shaping of pure forms. What interests him, for the simple joy of his own artistic fulfillment, is the search

for a plastic structure. In short, the cultural affinities and inspiration of Marini's work as well as the aims he follows are all one. His work, besides, is limited to three or four subjects or, even better, three or four "motifs." It is precisely these "motifs" that enable him to avoid falling into the traps of an anecdotal or decorative style. Despite the apparent poverty of his themes, he has given proof of great imagination, an imagination that leads him not so much toward the "subject" as toward a formal research concerned with rhythms, volumes and lines. As for his spontaneity, it is often the fruit of much work and of culture that has been carefully assimilated. In other words, the theme that Marini choses to develop only serves as the pretext for a series of works each one of which must represent an advance over the preceding one. The starting point may be no more than a simple, very elementary sketch which goes through a process of continuous enrichment. This is why certain works might seem to be slightly bitter, a trifle acid to the taste of the superficial observer ...

*From* Marino Marini *(Florence: Ed. U., 1946).*

Enzo Carli:
# THE THEMES OF MARINI

... Some people have reproached Marino Marini for the thematic poverty of his iconography. In fact, this supposed poverty is only the direct consequence and the most obvious proof of his search for the absolute. It is well-known that almost all of the sculptor's work can be cataloged under three very general titles: the female nude, usually seen standing up, the horse with or without a rider, and the portrait, most frequently a single head, and occasionally nothing but a mask. Rare are the subjects that do not fall under one of the above headings. Personally I find that whenever Marini has given his work a more or less suggestive title, it seems to create a dissonance, even

more, it weakens the effective scope of the work. It is not really important to know that the thin character that belongs to the Kunstmuseum in Basel is an Archangel, or that some other magnificent image belongs to the Jesi collection. There is a much more radical criterion: when a portrait, even if it bears a close resemblance to the model, succeeds in imposing itself upon the viewer by the sole force of its abstract power. This is exactly what happens with many of Marini's more hallucinatory *Riders* ...

*From* Marino Marini *(Milan: Ed. Hoepli, 1950).*

*(Photo Maria Netter, Basel).* ▷

# A.M. Hammacher:
# MAKING A PORTRAIT

... Making a portrait, for Marino Marini, has always been, finally, the equivalent of making a sculpture. As the artist's hand enters into contact with planes and volumes, the qualities of sculptural form, properly speaking, are little by little affirmed. The "heads" sometimes evoke mountains, sometimes a Vulcan, or else a Pompeian beauty, or even a life that has been consumed with passion. The faces show a wide range of expressions: lassitude, sadness, tenderness, or else attentiveness, irony, drollery, expressions which have their source in life itself.

If it is true that Despiau was able to discern in man those qualities that make him cultured and refined, it can be said that Marino Marini, moving around his sculptures in the fashion of a mime, reveals those aspects of his models that are most singular, most violently accentuated in a physical and moral sense. This is why his portraits never seek to please; they are faces that have been more unmasked than flattered. They are not, however, caricatures. The artist has too much respect for the human person. He is incapable of fixing his models, of embalming them for eternity. He shapes them rather such as they emerged from the maternal womb and such also as life has shaped them. No other artist of his time has been so successful in revealing the spirit of his contemporaries. But we should not make the mistake of believing that these portraits are only simple objective representations devoid of art. The secret of Marini's work lies in the artist's ability to "project" himself in his models and to do this without any narcissism. When a model poses for Marini, what takes place is more than a simple and mechanical professional formality. On the contrary, a complicity is established, and Marini's "look" forces the "otherness" of the model to merge with his vision, whereas he himself keeps, intangible, his own personality ...

*From* Marino Marini, Sculpture, Painting, Drawing *(London: Thames and Hudson Publishers, 1971).*

With the publisher Gottfried B. Fischer (1967).

With Mies Van Der Rohe (1967). (*Photos Marina Marini*).

Portrait of Igor Stravinsky (2nd version). 1951. Bronze. Height: 12 ⁵/₈". Galleria Civica d'Arte Moderna, Milan.

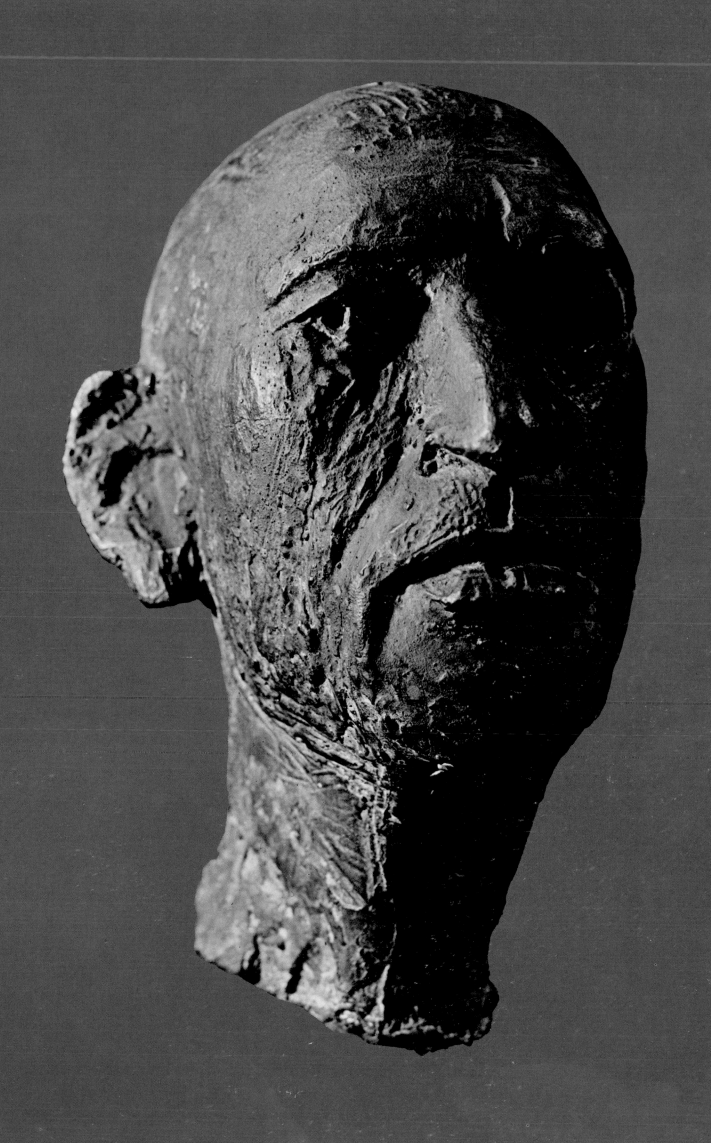

Portrait of Germaine Richier. 1945. Plaster. Height: 13″. Galleria Civica d'Arte Moderna, Milan.

# Werner Hofmann:
# A PLASTIC DRAMATIZATION

... The war, finally, acted as a stimulus on Marino Marini. It helped free his expressive language of any idyllic mediocrity and was responsible for the passionate, discordant notes he began to strike. It was only after the war that his women attained their full femininity and that his men likewise attained their maximum virility.

This differentiation of the sexes went hand in hand with a more precise plastic dramatization. A strict linear discipline alternated with an intense use of color. The formal structure was endowed with a polyphonic movement and was infused with passion. This period has been aptly referred to as Marini's "Neo-Expressionism." It began in 1946 and coincided approximately with Marini's return to Italy. The development can be easily seen in the study for a *Rider* "with his arms stretched out." The horse looks as if it might have been drawn by Paolo Uccello. It is a stocky, robust animal standing on three legs, imprinted in relief, and is surmounted by a figure that looks as if it were hooded with a sack. The body of this figure is sunken into the animal's. Its short, massive arms are stretched out in a questioning way and the head is sharply raised upward. The early fluidity has disappeared. Now the limbs are hard and solid. They are transfixed with sudden emotion. Here and there, however, the old, more supple graphic style can be distinguished. It is covered with extremely dense crosshatchings that blot out the impasto left by the brush. It is in this way that the compact and massive structure emerges. A feeling of magic emanates from this *Rider*.

Its apparent lack of life, its archaism, keeps the expression of this equestrian couple from being tinted with any pronounced "expressionism." What we see here is the incantatory moment on the road to Damas when a voice was heard saying: "You must change your life."

It is this new obligation that Marini's hand expresses. His gesture becomes abrupt and spasmodic. The chiaroscuro is torn with harsh contrasts. The corrosive pen bites and violates the paper. A brutal horizontal brushstroke, like a long lance, offers the only visible resistance to the oblique, convulsive forms on the right. But the real reason for the tension that grips both man and animal is not something artificial, neither an abyss nor a bar-

rier, but an inner obstacle. The preceding riders had a peaceful look about them and bore witness to their real mastery over their mount. They sat firmly on the curved line of the horse's hindquarters. Now, however, the two

bodies are joined in the same oblique/vertical movement. Under the weight of the common menace, horse and rider are forced to become allies ...

*From* L'Opera grafica di Marino Marini *(Milan: Ed. Il Saggiatore, 1960).*

With Noguchi (1964).

With Henry Miller (1961). (*Photos Marina Marini*).

With Henry Moore (1961).

With Lipchitz (1962). (*Photos Marina Marini*).

## Alberto Busignani:
# A WITNESS OF HIS TIME

...After the second *Miracle*, Marini boldly sought to explore the mysteries of human existence, incessantly confronting the "everyday" world with the eternal "myths." Out of this came that many-layered work which gradually, in time, has been enriched by new facets; this is especially true if one goes back to the distant period when he sculpted *The People* (1929). In this context it is perhaps worthwhile to recall the second *Ersilia* of 1949 which recapitulates the theme of the thirties. This theme has been held onto with such perseverance that it seems to form a part of the sculpture, whereas in reality the sculpture is the double result of, on the one hand, the dramatic events of 1943 and, on the other, the fertile years that followed 1946. Regardless of whether it is a question of a poor girl or of the "Demoiselles d'Avignon," of whether it is a question of the myth of the "lady" or of a woman marked by all the experiences of life, Marini infallibly arrives at the archetype of woman in her majesty (as a contemporary Giotto would). We find here a whole network of meaning, an extremely beautiful symbolic system for our time.

As for Marini's more recent works, it is conceivable that we are all too implicated in their history. A long discourse would risk involving us in a sort of involuntary autobiography or else it would engage us in a too formalistic description that would force us to make inconsiderate judgements about

"abstraction" or "expressionism." Let us thus limit ourselves to commenting upon a few of the major characteristics of Marini's work; in other words, let us recall a few of the criticisms that have already been made. What should be underlined then, above all, is the great structural principle that governs the whole of Marini's work, from the theme of the *Rider*, by way of the second *Miracle*, to the grand theme of the *Warrior* as it is shown in the group of 1959-60 or as it reappears in the extraordinary carving of 1967 (the first sketch, *Idea for the Warrior*, dates from 1956), and which is constantly renewed in a series of creations.

The large stone *Warrior* of 1967 provides ample confirmation of Marini's constant evolution. What is significant is that this evolution always seems to be intuitively and deliberately linked to a fundamental concept about man. Whether it is embodied in the skillful simplicity of the *Riders* or in the tragic sense of the *Miracles*, whether is reaches its greatest profundity in the *Warriors* or assumes a convulsive aspect in the almost universal psychology of the "portraits," Marini's inspiration has always been and still remains "human." That is to say, it is grounded and has its source in the human element, be that element divine or monstrous, olympian or burned by the flames of everyday purgatory, in happiness as in adversity.

Is there any need, furthermore, to specify that the word "myth," so often

used in relation to Marini, should not be understood in the sense of an anecdotal or moralistic fable but in the sense of a symbol nourished both by contemporary events and by lived reminiscences? In fact, beyond the more or less exterior or occasional references to what is called "culture," Marini, throughout his development, has always insisted upon and highlighted the wholeness and immediacy of human values. These values, thanks to the artist, are transmuted into poetic evidence. The resonances they arouse in the viewer are based on their subtle correspondences with Etruscan clay, Gothic stone, prehistoric lava or Greek marble. In short, history is not divorced from the contemporary world.

But what is the true impact of the artist on his contemporaries? This is a question that it is not easy to answer with certitude. The response, besides, risks to be very disturbing. One fact, however, is incontestable: the monuments at The Hague or at Rotterdam exist, and the simple fact of their presence testifies to the relationship that is inevitably formed between the artist and the people. This serves to confirm that Marini's deepest intentions find an echo beyond the limits of frontiers. There is no doubt that Marini is a witness of his time. Who knows whether his work does not even contain, here and there, some prophetic element ...

*From* Marino Marini *(Florence: Ed. Sansoni, 1968)*.

Franco Russoli:
# THE ÉLAN OF THE "WARRIORS"

... In 1959 and 1960 Marino Marini made several sketches and sculptures of varying sizes that he called *Warriors*. In them the artist reached his highest degree of poetic intensity. The horse looks as if it had been struck by lightning. It stumbles and falls to its knees. Its head is twisted back and its torn, emaciated nostrils are flared upwards. Breathless, man is flattened out against the animal. He hangs on desperately and screams. The horse's head is crushed and covered with wounds. The horse looks back at its unknown enemy and its companion in wretchedness.

Horse and rider no longer really exist in themselves. They are merged together in a block of consumed matter, of primordial structures and petrified bones. There is a terrible, bursting, convulsive power to the collapsing architecture that they form. This power is so organic, so related to life, that it is far removed from any abstract composition in a Cubist manner. The forms develop directly out of the meaning of the image, and that meaning has a moral, not aesthetic, content. It is a chapter in human history. This is why it is impossible to fully understand and appreciate this sculpture if

an abstraction is made of its meaning and if one looks only at formal considerations. For example, the diagonal line along which the bodies are stretched, the way the heads and limbs diverge from this basic directional axis, is a brilliant transcription, in plastic terms, of a real gesture.

The penetrating observation of reality is also responsible for the quality of the fantastic and expressive transfiguration ...

*From* Marino Marini's Warrior, *XXᵉ siècle no. 21, Paris, 1963.*

With his sister Egle Marini (1960). (*Photo Marina Marini*).

With Jean Arp (1963).

## Franco Russoli:
# THE PAINTER AND THE SCULPTOR

... For Marino Marini, painting is an art that transforms the physical substance of the object into pure symbols, as it translates sensory elements into chromatic, plastic and linear values. Each and every one of Marini's works is always endowed with a specific meaning, that is to say it is always adapted to the technique the artist has chosen.

. . . . . . . . . . . . .

As for Marini's drawing, at the time when the artist returned to a sort of Neo-Classicism, the stylized line still continued to thrive in the delicate atmosphere of a romantic light. A little like Carrà in relation to Ranzoni. But there is something fresher, more sen-

sual, for example, in the way the hands are dimpled and in the fleshy outline of the mouth. Later on the structural element characteristic of Tuscany in the twentieth-century became more accentuated; this element, in Soffici's work, does not lose anything of its bourgeois savor, although the formal rigor is conserved. It is thus that the timid, almost languid, *Young Girl with a Flower* appeared in 1926. But Marini's need to restitute all their density to beings and things, without any sophistication or reference to academic norms, soon asserted itself. *The Algerian Woman* (1927) is a good example of this and announces certain ironic and sensual works of the Roman school. This realism, this intuition of the "typical" character of his models, at once spontaneous and free, full of humor and pathos, can also be found in the Etruscans, whose art is one of his sources and of whom he considers himself the heir.

This is apparent in the terracotta *The People* and in the picture *Violetta* (1928). There is a concerted violence in Marini's rendering of these works, in the way he shapes the masses in a simple and unaffected composition, and in the broad way he models these robust, popular figures who are filled with an ancient pride.

. . . . . . . . . . . . .

Starting in 1948, Marini undertook many canvases. This activity, however, did not hurt his work as a sculptor. It is even possible to pick out the affinities that exist between his pictures and his sculptures. His recent work expresses a new requirement. He starts out from elements that are immediately given, sometimes volumes, sometimes flat images. As for his private symbolic universe—his nudes, jugglers, riders—it is obvious that Marini has used them to his advantage but not in the manner of some seductive stylistic conceit. His symbolism seeks to depict the human "types" that are especially representative of our troubled times. These "models" have occasionally given rise to many different interpretations, but it is certain that they do not exist only in function of abstract imperatives. On the contrary, Marini never loses sight of the necessity for a thematic coherence that faithfully reflects the chosen mode of expression. The fact that he is attracted now by realism, now by archaism and even by Cubism, or that his energy draws him toward the primitive "magma," should be seen as a sign of his never-ending interest in the human adventure ...

*From* Marino Marini, Dipinti e Disegni *(Milan: Toninelli Ed., 1963).*

Umbro Apollonio:
# THE CONTEMPORARY RELEVANCE OF MARINI

... Is Marini a traditional sculptor? Or is his work timeless in the sense that it belongs as much to the art of the past as to the art of today? Is his art intended only for museums? Perhaps. But what form of art has not, at one time or another, and long before the epoch of Cézanne, pretended to make its entry in the museum? All things considered, the contemporary relevance of Marini is beyond doubt. Each of his works is vitally concerned with the question of man and awakes immemorial sensations. Each of his works as well has an existential truth in which the presence of the individual can invariably be felt.

In times as ephemeral as our own, Marini has touched upon everything that is hidden in the depths of the human being, whether pathetic or lyrical. The proof of this is his "portraits." Whatever level of formal success they achieve, it cannot be denied that they constitute a true means of communication and stimulate and bring into focus all of man's lyrical powers. Pure plasticism and color are coordinated so well together that they bring forth an abstraction that in itself represents a new and vital historical form. Finally, what characterizes Marini's contribution is a sort of constant resurrection of tradition which is more and more closely confronted with contemporary reality in order to better explore the labyrinth of human complexity. In this way each moment of the present becomes, at one and the same time, a "memory" of the past and a clarion call tirelessly announcing man's future ...

*From* Marino Marini *(Milan: Ed. del Milione, 1953; third edition of 1958 brought up to date).*

Left to right: G. di San Lazzaro, Marini and Arturo Bassi, at the opening of the six rooms devoted to Marino Marini at the Galleria Civica d'Arte Moderna of Milan (1973). (*Photo Marina Marini*).

At the Mourlot workshop (1968).

# Giovanni Carandente:
# THE LITHOGRAPHS

... There are many ways in which Marini's graphic and sculptural work are related, and this is true from his first works of a simple pictorial inspiration to the most plastically symbolic studies that are quickly traced on a sheet of paper and then transferred to stone. In both cases, however, it is the plastic element that dominates and that stands out, peremptory, rich with all of the artist's moods and that special vitality that makes Marini one of the greatest creators of forms of our time. There is no doubt that Marini's lithographic output, which is spread over twenty years, has not the quantitative importance of that of Picasso or Braque, but it is marked by an unvaryingly high quality. Volume and movement have always constituted for Marini the two primordial components of expression. His works are first of all remarkable for their sculptural immobility and their immanent human presence. Then there is the tension of the bodies which are articulated in space with an ever increasing movement and aggressiveness ...

*From* The Lithographs of Marino Marini *(Milan: Toninelli Ed., 1966).*

At Querceta in the Henraux workshops (1971). ▷
*(Photo Luigi Beggi).*

130

The artist and his wife at Forte dei Marmi.

## Carlo Pirovano:
# THE MEANING OF AN ŒUVRE

... Once again we are led to ask: what are the interpretations that the œuvre of Marino Marini gives rise to? Undoubtedly his interest in archaic art, which was apparent from the very beginning, constituted a defensive attitude on the part of the artist. But the result was that the true symbolism of each of his works was misunderstood on account of the familiar intellectual prejudice that consists in attributing to plastic works meanings that are either too philosophical or too metaphysical.

There is absolutely nothing pseudo-metaphysical about Marini. Even less is there anything of those Freudian exercises dear to the Surrealists. His work is, above all, flesh, blood and nerves. The rest comes afterwards.

. . . . . . . . . . . . .

The third period of his work marks the point when Marini began to develop the epic symphony of horse and rider. At this time the classicism in his work was slowly modified, and there was a progressive emphasis on plastic density which was articulated in a much more complex spatial organization.

In other words, if we were to make an abstraction of the figurative and symbolical aspects of his work and were only to transcribe, like the ideograms of computers, the spatial tensions, we would have, in the *Riders* that were done prior to 1950, a vertical line on a horizontal line, and in the *Miracles*, two diagonals, contrasted, but with a clear tendency to merge ...

*From* Marino Marini Sculptore *(Milan: Electa Editrice, 1972).*

# Biography

**1901** On February 27 Marino Marini and his twin sister Egle were born at Pistoia in Tuscany. His parents lived in a house near the church of San Pietro.

**1915** Marini met Rodin, who was travelling in Italy and had stopped in Florence to look again at the works of Donatello and Michelangelo.

**1917** Marini and his sister Egle enrolled at the Academy of Fine Arts in Florence to take courses in painting and sculpture.

**1919** Marini attended the painting classes given by Galileo Chini.

**1922** Marini, without giving up painting, chose sculpture as his medium of expression and studied with Domenico Trentacosta.

**1923** He participated in the II Biennale in Rome.

**1926** His first workshop and his first series of *Portraits*.

**1927** He participated in the III International Exhibition of Decorative Arts in Monza.

**1928** His first trip to Paris. His first group show at the Galleria Milano, Milan.

**1929** The sculptor Arturo Martini invited Marini, who accepted, to take over his professorship in sculpture at the School of Fine Arts of the Villa Royale in Monza. Exhibitions of the Italian Novecento in Nice and Milan. The artist executed *People*.

**1930** Stay in Paris. He met Campigli, De Chirico, Magnelli and De Pisis as well as Gonzales, Kandinsky and Maillol. Group exhibitions at the Kunsthalle in Bern and at the Kunstmuseum in Basel.

**1931** Stay in Paris. Exhibition of the Italian Novecento in Stockholm. The artist executed *Ersilia*.

**1932** First one-man shows at the Galleria Milano, Milan and the Galleria Sabatello, Rome. Exhibited for the first time at the Venice Biennale. Became an honorary member of the Florentine Academy of the Arts. Start of the series of *Jugglers*.

**1933** Exhibited with Campigli at the Galleria Milano and participated in the V Triennale of Milan where he received a diploma and a Silver Medal.

**1934** Trip to Frankfurt, Nuremberg and Bamberg as well as to Rome, Venice and Padua. XIX Venice Biennale.

**1935** Trip to Greece. Awarded the First Sculpture Prize at the II Quadriennale of Rome. Start of the series of *Pomonas*.

**1936** Stay in Paris. Met and became friendly with Picasso, Braque, Laurens. First monograph on his work published in "Chroniques du Jour" (Paris: G. di San Lazzaro Ed.).

**1937** Awarded the "Grand Prix" of the International Exhibition in Paris. One-man show at the Galleria Barbaroux, Milan.

**1938** Marini married a young Swiss girl from the Tessin, Mercedes Pedrazzini, whom he rebaptized Marina.

**1939** Start of the series of *Dancers*.

**1940** Marini left his classes at Monza in order to teach at the Brera Academy in Milan. Exhibition of his sculptures along with other Italian artists at the Kunsthaus in Zurich.

**1941** His studio and his works were destroyed by bombs. Marini and his wife left for Switzerland and settled at Tenero-Locarno in the Tessin. One-man shows in Genoa, Rome and Venice. Frequent stays in Basel and Zurich where he met Germaine Richier, Otto Bänninger, Fritz Wotruba, Giacometti, Habacher, H. Haller.

**1943** The artist executed *Archangel*. Start of the series of *Miracles*.

**1944** Participated in the exhibition "Four Foreign Sculptors in Switzerland" at the Kunstmuseum in Basel.

**1945** Exhibited with Germaine Richier and Fritz Wotruba at the Kunsthalle in Bern. One-man shows in Basel and Zurich.

**1946** Marini returned to Italy and settled in Milan.

**1947** Became corresponding member of the Accademia Clementina, Bologna.

**1948** Met the well-known American art dealer, Curt Valentin. Participated in the XXIV Venice Biennale (where he had his own room) and met H. Moore.

**1949** One-man show in Rome. The artist executed *The Angel of the City*.

**1950** First one-man show in the U.S.A. at the Buchholz Gallery (Curt Valentin) in New York and his first trip to the U.S.A. where he met Lipchitz, Arp, Calder, Beckmann, Tanguy, Feininger and Stravinsky, whose portrait he made.

**1951** Before returning to Milan, Marini stopped in London where the Hanover Gallery organized an exhibition of his sculptures and drawings. One-man show at the Kestner Gesellschaft in Hanover. Became honorary member of the Akademisches Kollegium, Munich.

**1952** Awarded the First Sculpture Price at the XXVI Venice Biennale (his own room). One-man show at the Kunstverein in Hamburg and at the Bayerische Staatsgemaldesammlungen in Munich. Together with Moore and Wotruba exhibited at the Galerie Welz in Salzburg. Member of the Kunglige Akademien for de Fria Konsterna, Stockholm.

**1953** Travelling exhibition in Swedish, Danish and Norwegian museums: Göteborg, Stockholm, Copenhagen and Oslo. One-man show at the Cincinnati Art Museum and at the Buchholz Gallery in New York. Participated in the II International Open-Air Sculpture Biennial, Middelheim Park, Antwerp, and in the II Biennial of Sao Paulo. Marini purchased a house at Forte dei Marmi, near Carraro. Curt Valentin died there the same year.

**1954** One-man shows in Helsinki, Geneva, Bern, Cologne, Basel and Zurich. Participated in the International Open-Air Exhibition of Sculptures in London. Awarded the International Grand Prize of the Accademia dei Lincei of the city of Rome as well as the Gold Medal of the President of the Republic. Became honorary member of the International Mark Twain Society, Kirkwood, Missouri.

**1955** One-man shows in the museums of Rotterdam, Düsseldorf and Mannheim. Participated in the III Middelheim Park Biennial at Antwerp, in the International Exhibition Documenta I at Kassel and in the International Exhibition of the Carnegie Institute in Pittsburgh. One-man show at the Martha Jackson Gallery and at the Pierre Matisse Gallery in New York.

**1956** Participated in the International Exhibition at Recklinghausen and in the International Exhibition of Sculpture at the Musée Rodin in Paris. Start of the series of *Warriors*.

**1957** One-man show in New York at The Contemporaries Gallery and in Düsseldorf at the Galerie Vömel. Member of the Accademia Nazionale de San Lucca, Rome.

**1958** One-man show at the Pierre Matisse Gallery in New York and in Lausanne. Corresponding member of the Bayerische Akademie der Schönen Künste, Munich.

**1959** The artist's largest bronze sculpture, *Equestrian Composition*, was erected at the Hague. Participated in the V Open-Air Sculpture Biennial at Middelheim Park in Antwerp, in the III International Exhibition of Engraving at Ljubljana and in Documenta II at Kassel. Active member, Accademia Latinitati, Excolendæ, Rome. Corresponding member, Academia Nacional de Belles Artes, Buenos Aires.

**1961** Participated in the VI Biennial at Middelheim Park in Antwerp, in the VI Biennial in Tokyo and in the International Exhibition of the Carnegie Institute in Pittsburgh. Awarded the Donatello Prize of the city of Florence. Member of the Pontificia Insigne Accademia Artistica dei Virtuosi, Rome.

**1962** First large retrospective at the Kunsthaus in Zurich. Participated in the International Exhibition of Sculpture in Spoleto and in the XXXI Venice Biennale. Awarded the Gold Medal for Merit of the Commune of Milan. Became honorary member of the Accademia 500 in Rome and honorary member of the Akademie der Bildenden Künste in Nuremberg. Start of the series of *Cries*. The artist executed the *Great Cry*.

**1963** One-man show of paintings at the Galerie Günther Franks in Munich. Retrospective at the Museum Boymans-Van Beuningen in Rotterdam. Participated in the VIII International Exhibition of White and Black in Lugano, in the XXXII Venice Biennale, in Documenta III at Kassel and in the International Exhibition of the Carnegie Institute in Pittsburgh. Awarded the "Europa Arte" Prize of the city of Ancona.

**1965** Exhibition of paintings at the Musée Royal des Beaux-Arts in Antwerp and of graphic works at the Philadelphia Museum of Art. Honorary associate, Associazione Incisori d'Italia, Turin-Milan-Rome.

**1966** Large retrospective at the Palazzo Venezia in Rome. Travelling exhibition of paintings and drawings at Darmstadt, Nuremberg and Kaiserlautern. Awarded the "Ibico Reggino" Prize by Reggio Calabria. Member of the Instituto Accademico, Rome.

**1967** Exhibition of paintings at the Galleria Toninelli in Milan. Participated in the International Exhibition of Contemporary Sculpture in Montreal, in the International Exhibition of Engraving at Vancouver, in the International Exhibition of Sculpture at the Guggenheim Museum in New York and in the International Exhibition of the Carnegie Institute in Pittsburgh. Awarded the Gold Medal of Acknowledgement of the city of Florence, the Biancamano Prize of the city of Milan, the Gold Medal of Great Civic Merit of the Chamber of Commerce in Pistoia. Honorary member of the Accademia Clementina, Bologna.

**1968** One-man show at the Weintraub Gallery in New York. Participated in the International Exhibition of Graphic Art at the Palazzo Strozzi in Florence. Awarded first prize at the VIII Biennale of Contemporary Italian Engravers by the Commune of Venice. Became an honorary member of the American Academy of Arts and Letters, New York; honorary member of the National Institute of Arts and Letters, New York; honorary member of the Accademia Pistoiese del Ceppo, Pistoia; member of the Order für Wissenschaft und Künste "For Merit," Göttingen.

1969 Exhibition of a portfolio of lithographs published by XXᵉ siècle "From Color to Form" at the Bibliothèque Nationale, Paris. Exhibition of graphic works in Hamburg and London. Awarded the Medal of the Presidency of the Italian Chamber of Deputies. Appointed Knight of the International Mark Twain Society, Kirkwood, Missouri, and honorary member of the Brigata del Leoncino, Cultural Association of Pistoia.

1970 One-man show of paintings, drawings, and then of thirty-three etchings at the Galleria Toninelli in Milan. Participated in the II International Biennale of Graphic Art at the Palazzo Strozzi in Florence and in the International Art Fair at Basel. Honorary member of the International Union of Peace, Presidential Seat, Turin.

1971 Exhibition of graphic works in Rome, Milan, Frankfurt, Livorno, Düsseldorf and at the Galerie XXᵉ siècle in Paris. Participated in the Venice Biennale. Awarded the "Perseo d'Oro" Prize of the city of Florence. Became a member of the "Guglielmo Marconi" Universal Academy, Rome.

1972 Exhibition of *Portraits* "Personages of the 20th Century" at the Piero della Francesca Study Center in Milan. All these sculptures were donated by Marini a year later to the Museum of Modern Art in Milan. Became an honorary citizen of the city of Milan on March 27. Awarded the "Il Cino" Prize of the city of Pistoia.

1973 Gianni Agnelli purchased the stone *Miracle* of 1970-71 and gave it to the Vatican which inaugurated its Museum of Modern Art in June. Marini participated in the International Open-Air Exhibition of Sculpture "Città - Spazio - Sculture" at Rimini. On December 13 the Museum of Modern Art of Milan (formerly Villa Reale) opened. Six of its rooms are devoted to the *Portraits* ("Personages of the 20th Century") donated by Marini and to works from the collection of Marina Marini—sculptures, paintings, engravings, lithographs and drawings—that are on loan to the museum. Awarded the Gold Medal of the city of Rimini and the Gold Medal for "The Versilia" along with Lipchitz and Moore.

# Monographs

1936 - Paul Fierens
*Marino Marini (Art Italien Moderne)*, Chroniques du Jour. Paris, Hoepli, Milan.

1937 - Lamberto Vitali
*Marino Marini (Arte Moderna Italiana)*, Hoepli, Milan.

1939 - G. Cesetti
*Marino Marini (Quaderni del Disegno)*, Ed. del Cavallino, Venice.

1941 - Filippo De Pisis
*Marino Marini*, Ed. della Conchiglia, Milan.

1942 - L. Anceschi
*Marino Marini (Quaderni del Disegno Contemporaneo)*, Ed. della "Galleria della Spiga e Corrente," Milan.

1944 - G. Contini
*20 sculture di Marino Marini*, Ed. della Collana, Lugano.

1946 - Lamberto Vitali
*Marini (Quaderni d'Arte a cura di G. Raimondi e di C.L. Ragghianti)*, Ed. U., Florence.

1948 - Raffaele Carrieri
*Marino Marini*, Ed. del Milione, Milan.

1950 - Enzo Carli
*Marino Marini (Arte Moderna Italiana)*, Hoepli, Milan.

1951 - Mario Ramous
*Marino Marini*, Cappelli, Bologna.

1951 - Mario Ramous
*Marino Marini, Due litografie e sei disegni*, Cappelli, Bologna.

1953 - Umbro Apollonio
*Marino Marini*, Ed. del Milione, Milan, 2nd and 3rd editions revised.

1954 - Eduard Trier.
*Marino Marini, Galerie Der Spiegel*, Cologne.
*Marino, sei tavole a colori*, Ed.

1954 - Sinagra (E. Marini)
del Milione, Milan.

1954 - Emil Langui
*Marini*, Albert de Lange, Amsterdam.

1959 - Douglas Cooper
*Marino Marini*, Silvana editoriale d'Arte, Milan.

1959 - Egle Marini
*Marino Marini*, der Arche, Zurich.

1960 - P. M. Bardi
*Marini - Graphic Work and Paintings*, Harry N. Abrams, New York.

1960 - Werner Hofmann
*Marini - Malerei und Graphik*, Gerd Hatje, Stuttgart.

1960 - Werner Hofmann
*L'opera grafica di Marino Marini*, Il Saggiatore, Milan.

1961 - Egle Marini
*Marino Marini - Ein Lebensbild, ein Gesprach mit seiner Schwester Egle*, Fischer Bücherei, Frankfurt-am-Main.

1961 - Eduard Trier
*Marino Marini*, Gerd Hatje, Stuttgart.

1961 - Eduard Trier
*Marino Marini*, Garzanti, Milan.

1961 - Eduard Trier
*Marino Marini*, Ed. du Griffon, Neuchatel.

1961 - Eduard Trier
*Marino Marini*, Praeger, New York.

1961 - Heinz Fuchs
*Il Miracolo - Marino Marini*, Ed. Philipp Reclam Jr., Stuttgart.

1961 - Eduard Trier
*The Sculpture of Marino Marini*, Thames and Hudson, London.

1963 - Hartmut Biermann
*Marino Marini* - Deutsche Buch Gemeinschaft Berlin-Darmstadt-Vienna.

1963 - Hartmut Biermann
*Marino Marini*, Emil Vollmer, Wiesbaden, Berlin.

1963 - Franco Russoli
*Il Guerriero di Marino Marini*, Aldo Martello, Milan.

1963 - Franco Russoli
*Marino Marini - Dipinti e disegni*, Toninelli, Milan.

1964 - Franco Russoli
*Marino Marini - Paintings and Drawings*, Harry N. Abrams, New York.

1964 - Franco Russoli
*Marino Marini - Bilder und Zeichnungen*, Gerd Hatje, Stuttgart.

1964 - Franco Russoli
*Marino Marini - Paintings and Drawings*, Thames and Hudson, London.

1966 - Giovanni Carandente
*Le Litografie di Marino Marini*, Toninelli, Milan.

1966 - Jiri Setlik
*Marini*, Odeon, Prague.

1966 - Giovanni Carandente
*Marino Marini (I Maestri della Scultura)*, Fratelli Fabbri, Milan.

1968 - Alberto Busignoni
*Marino Marini*, Sadea Sansoni, Florence.

1968 - Giovanni Carandente
*Marino Marini. Lithographs 1942-1965*, Harry N. Abrams, New York.

1968 - Werner Haftmann
*Marino Marini: Werk Ausgabe*, Carl Schünemann, Bremen.

1969 - Werner Haftmann
*Marino Marini. A suite of sixty-three re-creations of drawings and sketches*, Harry N. Abrams, New York.

1970 - Patrick Waldberg, Herbert Read, G. di San Lazzaro
*L'Œuvre complet de Marino Marini*, Ed. XXᵉ siècle, Paris.

1970 - Patrick Waldberg, Herbert Read, G. di San Lazzaro
*L'Opera completa di Marino Marini*, Silvana Editoriale d'Arte, Milan.

1970 - Patrick Waldberg, Herbert Read, G. di San Lazzaro
*Complete Works of Marino Marini*, Tudor Publishing Co., New York.

1971 - Patrick Waldberg, Herbert Read, G. di San Lazzaro
*Marino Marini, Leben und Werk, Gesamtkatalog*, Propyläen Verlag, Berlin.

1971 - Oskar Bätschmann
*Marino Marini*, Kunstkreis, Lucerne.

1971 - A. M. Hammacher
*Marino Marini, Sculpture, Painting, Drawing*, Harry N. Abrams, New York.

1971 - A. M. Hammacher
*Marino Marini, Sculpture, Painting, Drawing*, Thames and Hudson, London.

1972 - A. M. Hammacher
*Marino Marini, Skulptur, Malerei, Zeichnung*, Carl Schünemann Verlag, Bremen.

1972 - Alberto Busignani
*Marino Marini*, Hamlyn, London.

1972 - Ernesto Caballo
*Marino Marini. Diario fotografica di raccontato da Marina con pensieri di Marino e liriche di Egle Marini*. Albra Editrice, Turin.

1972 - Azuma
*Marino Marini*, Heibonska Ltd, Tokyo.

1972 - Marina Marini
*Marino Marini. Biografia per immagini*, Albra Editrice, Turin.

1972 - Carlo Pirovano
*Marino Marini Sculptore*, Electa Editrice, Milan.

# Graphic Works and Illustrated Books

1942 - Ugo Foscolo
*Ultime lettere di Jacopo Ortis*, Ed. della Conchiglia, Milan. (Drawings).

1942 - Salvatore Quasimodo
*Il fiore delle Georgiche*, Ed. della Conchiglia, Milan. (Drawings).

1951 - Mario Ramous
*La memoria, il messaggio*, Ed. Cappelli, Bologna (Drawings).

1957 - Egle Marini
*Poesie*, Ed. Del Milione, Milan. (Drawings).

1958 - Egle Marini
*Gedichte*, Fischer, Frankfurt-am-Main. (Drawings).

1963 - Egle Marini
*Idea e Spazio* - 12 original etchings. "Les Cent Bibliophiles de France et d'Amérique," Paris.

1968 - G. di San Lazzaro
*L'Album Nº 1*. 12 original etchings. XXᵉ siècle, Paris. Amiel, New York.

1969 - Marino Marini
*From Color to Form*. 10 original lithographs in color. XXᵉ siècle, Paris. Amiel, New York.

1970 - Douglas Cooper
*23 engravings of Marino Marini*. Crommelynck, Paris.

1970
*Imagines*. 10 original etchings, Propyläen Verlag, Berlin.

1971 - Egle Marini
*Tout près de Marino*, 10 original etchings, of which 8 in color, XXᵉ siècle, Paris.

1972 - Franco Russoli
*Marino Marini - Opera Grafica*, 20 original etchings and drypoints, Luigi De Tullio Publisher and Printer, Milan.

1972 - G. di San Lazzaro
*Chevaux et Cavaliers*, 8 original colored lithographs, XXᵉ siècle, Paris. Leon Amiel, New York.

1972 - Egle Marini
*Marino to Strawinsky*, 10 original engravings, of which 7 in color "etching, aquatint, drypoint," Albra Editrice, Turin.

1973 - Ada Negri
*Mein Thema*, 6 original etchings, Propyläen Verlag, Berlin.

1973 - Bernd Krimmel
*Selezione II*, 6 original etchings, Toninelli Arte Moderna Editore, Milan.

1973 - G. di San Lazzaro
*Personnages du Sacre du Printemps*, 8 original lithographs in color, XXᵉ siècle, Paris, Leon Amiel, New York.

# LEON AMIEL PUBLISHER INC., PARIS-NEW YORK

*JUST PUBLISHED:*

# MARINO MARINI

## *PERSONNAGES*
### *du*
## *SACRE DU PRINTEMPS*

With an Introduction by G. di San Lazzaro

8 original lithographs in color, 25 5/8″ × 19 3/4″, in a deluxe case.

- 10 copies on Japan paper numbered from I to X.
  3 nominative copies.
- 75 copies on Arches paper numbered from 1 to 75.
  25 copies H.C. numbered from H.C. I to H.C. XXV.

*All the plates are numbered and signed by the artist.*

*REMINDER:*

# MARINO MARINI

## *Complete Works*

by Patrick Waldberg

General catalogue of sculptures, paintings, engravings, lithographs
by G. di San Lazzaro
Introduction by Sir Herbert Read.

1969: first edition
1974: second enlarged edition

*More than 500 pages. Cloth-bound with a jacket especially designed by the artist.*
*1,000 reproductions, 80 of them in color.*

# LEON AMIEL PUBLISHER INC., PARIS-NEW YORK